8 TO BE GREAT
THE 8-TRAITS THAT LEAD TO GREAT SUCCESS

Richard St. John spent over 10 years interviewing 500 very successful people including many of the world's "Greats."

After analyzing every word they said, he discovered the core traits that lead to great success in any field. What he found might surprise you.

I've never seen a success book like this. It's incredible. I love everything about it, and that's saying something since I read for a living. This is such a fun, entertaining read and it's based on solid research. It really is a road map to greatness.

Louie Free host of The Louie Free Show, *Brainfood from the Heartland, syndicated radio*

It's fantastic. I've given it to everybody from colleagues at work to college kids and parents. Every one of them writes me and says, "What a great book." It's systematic and makes the intangible subject of success very tangible.

David M. Burk chairman, Clear Ink

I believe this book is going to be truly transformational and is going to change a lot of lives for the better.

Frank Borowicz lawyer, chairman of the Vancouver Board of Trade

It is a fantastic book. It brought about major changes in my life, and for my team at one of Mexico's largest banks. It proved to be a major way to enhance their motivation in work and in life.
Oscar Kaufmann president, Gcom-Kaufmann

My husband has never read a book in his life, except bedtime stories to the kids. But he picked up this book and has actually finished it. I'm thrilled!
Marnie Ballane director of business development, Speakers' Spotlight

This is one of the most entertaining books I have ever read. The writing is simple and concise, and the illustrations are captivating. Awesome!!
Mike Sporer owner, MS Consulting Associates

I gave the book to my son who is reflecting on his big life decisions. And he, surprisingly, did not hand it back to me. He even thanked me. How much better can it get?
Lois Frankel director, Carleton University

I don't like reading, but I liked this book. It made me feel like I can go far in life. My brain feels 3 times bigger.
Robert Ainsworth-Ferchat high school student

I have been in education a long time and I can't stress enough how well these ideas have been presented in a way that is a terrific platform for helping kids.
Randy Williams success teacher, Lester B. Pearson High School

Visit our website: **8ToBeGreat.com**
email: info@8ToBeGreat.com

---

8 To Be Great
Copyright © 2007 by Train of Thought Arts Inc.

8 To Be Great is a trademark of Train of Thought Arts Inc.
All Rights Reserved.

---

8 To Be Great
1st edition – includes index and sources.

ISBN 9780973900910

The author is human and makes mistakes. Just ask his wife. If you
discover mistakes, please contact us and we will make every effort to
make appropriate corrections.

This book is recyclable. Train of Thought Arts makes every effort to use
recycled paper, as well as ideas.

Train of Thought Arts Inc., 230 Niagara Street,
Toronto, ON, M6J 2L4, Canada

Printed in the United States of America

CONTENTS

What really leads to success?

This all started one day on a plane about 10 years ago. In the seat next to me was a teenage girl and she was really excited because it was her first plane ride. It looked to me like it might also be her last, because she came from a poor family, her parents were separating, and she was going to stay with relatives.

As I tapped away on my computer she kept asking me about my work. Then out of the blue she asked, "Are you successful?" I thought for a minute and said, "No, not really. Oprah, now there's a big success. Or my hero Terry Fox, a kid who ran thousands of miles on an artificial leg and raised millions for cancer research. Or Bill Gates, a guy who owns his own plane and doesn't have to sit next to some kid asking him questions." She laughed. But then I told her about some of my accomplishments in business and sports and she said, "I think you've been successful. So, are you a millionaire?"

I didn't know what to say. When I grew up it was bad manners to talk about money. But I figured I'd better be honest, and I said, "Yeah, I'm a millionaire, but I don't know how it happened. I didn't go after the money and it's not that important to me." She shot back, "Well, it's important to me. I don't want to be poor anymore. I want to get somewhere, but it's never gonna happen cause I'm not really smart. I'm not doin' great in school."

I said, "So what? I'm not smart. I barely made it through high school. I was never voted 'Most Popular' or 'Most Likely to Succeed.' Nobody thought I'd ever become successful, including me. I had nothing going for me, but I achieved success and also became a millionaire. So, if I can do it, you can do it." Then she hit me with the big question: "What really leads to success?" I said, "Sorry, I don't know. Somehow I just did it."

The plane landed and we said goodbye. I had a feeling she would do okay in life, but I felt bad that I couldn't help her more. I couldn't stop thinking, "How did a stupid guy like me, who barely passed high school, end up doing okay?" Then later, at a conference of the rich and famous, I was standing in a room surrounded by some of the world's great people when suddenly it hit me: "Why don't I ask them what led to their success?"

Now it's 10 years later, and I've interviewed more than 500 successful people and many of the world's "Greats." I've also sorted through thousands of interviews from other sources. The BIG job was taking all the information and analyzing and sorting it word by word, line by line, into all the factors that people said helped them succeed. Altogether I analyzed and sorted millions and millions of words.

Do you know how much work that is? I mean, it's all I've done, day and night, for over 10 years. The little project I thought would take a couple of months has consumed my life. I'll tell you, if I ever get my hands on that kid on the plane... Actually, if I do I'll thank her, because I've never met so many interesting people, and had so much fun!

And after all that work I discovered the *8 To Be Great – The 8-Traits That Lead to Great Success.* That's what this book is all about.

ABOUT THE **8 TO BE GREAT**
THE SECRET OF SUCCESS IS
THERE ARE NO SECRETS

My book *Stupid, Ugly, Unlucky, and RICH* showed that, contrary to popular belief, smarts, looks, and luck do NOT lead to success. Many great people aren't the smartest, or the best-looking, and they often have more bad luck than good. It's the 8-Traits that steer them to success, and that's what this book focuses on.

The *8 To Be Great* really are the key things that have taken the world's most successful people from the bottom to the top. But you could be thinking, "Wait a minute. These 8-Traits are all so simple. Passion, Work, Focus, Push, Ideas, Improve, Serve, and Persist are really common sense. Isn't there a 'secret' or something 'magical' that great people know about, and I don't?" Well, the answer is "No!"

The secret of success is: There are NO secrets. I've been studying this for over 10 years and the *8 To Be Great* are the foundation for success in any field. Other factors will also help us succeed, but if we don't have the 8-Traits we can try as many secrets as we want, and we still won't go far in life.

In my research I found hundreds of possible factors that lead to success, so how did I decide these 8 are the most important? Well, when I added up the quotes in my database, more people said these helped them succeed than anything else. Of course, technical skills, people skills, or communications skills will also help, depending on the field we're in, but if we want to succeed in any field we need the *8 To Be Great* as our foundation.

I didn't invent the 8-Traits. I don't own them. All successful people own them and always have. History shows these have been the constant keys to success throughout time. It's as if these are the 8 Laws of Success and they remain constant. It's nice to know that in a world that is forever changing, some things remain the same.

Every time I wash my car it will rain, and the *8 To Be Great* will always be the core for success.

And it's not just my humble opinion. This book is full of quotes from great people saying what helped them succeed, so you don't have to believe me, but do believe them. Also, the *8 To Be Great* have been thoroughly road-tested. Many successful people have seen my presentation and books and they confirm, "Yes! Those are what led to my success." Just a few examples:

Richard's 8-Traits for success are grounded in primary research, presented in a compelling original format, and are completely spot on. Torch your other success books.
Jonathan Sills senior VP, strategy & corporate development, ProFlowers

I believe what Richard says. His 8 factors are very consistent with what led to my success.
Arthur Benjamin math professor, "America's Best Math Whiz"

The author details 8 common sense factors underlying success. The factors are on the mark and not found in other business books. So if you are going to pick up one book, get this one.
David L. Anderson managing director, Supply Chain Ventures

The book really resonated with me. The principles in the book are what I believe in, what I've experienced, and what I try and teach my management team, as well as my kids.
Bill Strauss CEO, Provide-Commerce

So the secret of success is there are no secrets. I'm not saying success is simple, but the 8-Traits that lead to success are very simple to understand and easy to implement in your own life. These really are the 8 that make people great.

THE *8 TO BE GREAT* LEAD TO **SUCCESS AT ANYTHING**

FROM BEING A **ROCK STAR** TO **ROCKING YOUR BABY**

So there I was, sitting at Starbucks trying to come up with a good example to illustrate the *8 To Be Great*. My problem was too much choice. This book has hundreds of examples of great people in many different fields, so who should I pick? How about Bill Gates in technology? Maybe Oprah in entertainment? Or architect Frank Gehry? Or Martha Stewart?

I hate making these momentous decisions so I was really struggling. Plus, it was impossible to concentrate because there were all these kids running around. "Hey, what is this, Mother's Day at Starbucks?" And then it hit me — MOTHERS! A great Mother is a perfect example of somebody who constantly applies the top 8-Traits in her vocation of successfully raising a child.

PASSION

A great Mother loves her job as a mom and she has unconditional love for her child. Passion is an insufficient description of the way she feels. (Although it's not the same kind of passion that started it all.)

WORK

Mothering is all about work. The successful Mom works her butt off, especially in the beginning when it's 24-hour non-stop feeding and diaper changing. But there are also many giggles and grins, so it's work and fun all rolled into one.

FOCUS

A great Mother is more focused than a pilot landing a jumbo jet. Her child is all that matters in the world, and nothing will distract her from making sure that child lands safely in life.

PUSH

Mom keeps pushing herself to do stuff she really doesn't feel like doing, whether it's that 3 a.m. feeding or driving kids all over town. It's really double duty pushing, as she also helps her child push through barriers like shyness and doubt.

IMPROVE

A Mother has both herself and her child on a continuous improvement program. For her it's about getting better and better at parenting, and for her child it's about getting better at everything from school, to sports, to getting a date.

IDEAS

Mom is always coming up with ideas that solve dozens of day-to-day problems like how to get the puke stain out of the rug, or a good idea for her kid's next science project, speech, or Halloween costume.

SERVE

The successful Mother serves her child above all else, including herself. The little one comes first, she comes second. And a Mother never stops serving. Her kid can be 60 and Mom is still saying, "I just brought you a little something to eat."

PERSIST

A great Mother is a persistence machine, hanging in there through the whole life cycle of her child and persevering through the baby crap and the teenage crap, all the way to old age. And no matter what happens, she never, ever gives up on her kid.

Add it all up, and the 8-Traits are as essential to achieving success in raising a child as they are to success in any other vocation. And, although this book focuses mainly on the career side of life, keep in mind these traits also lead to success on the personal side. Whether it's marriage, parenting, relationships, hobbies, exercise, or health, the *8 To be Great* lead to success in any endeavor.

ABOUT THE **AUTHOR**

I really don't like talking about myself. "Yeah, sure. You'd never know it from this book!" However, I figure I have to tell you something about my background, because in the back of your mind you're probably thinking, "What credentials does this guy have to write a book on success?" And the answer is: I have no academic credentials. I barely passed high school and struggled through college. To top it off, I don't even look like a successful person – just your average, everyday guy. Yet I did achieve success in the real world, although not right away.

After graduating from design college, I traveled by bicycle through Asia for a year. Then I joined Nortel Networks' R&D labs where I spent my time bouncing from one thing to another: design, research, photography, advertising, producing videos, and writing. I could never figure out what title to put on my business card, so I just left it off. Finally I figured out what I really do. I'm a "De-mystic." I love researching and analyzing complex subjects, like technology, and then communicating them in a way that people can understand. After 10 good years of doing that at Nortel, I started my own company, and for 25 years we've helped large high-tech firms communicate to their customers through various media: video, print, TV, film, and the web. (Now comes the success stuff.)

In business for 25 years! Hey, that's a success. We've taken home some big awards, including the top ones in the world for best corporate videos and script-writing (at the Association for

Multi Image International Awards Festival in California). My photographs appeared in international publications and I even shot a cover for *Playboy*. But only once. My wife reminded me of that old Zen saying: "He who shoots bunnies could also get shot."

On the sports front, I've run a fairly fast marathon (26 miles or 42 km) in 2 hours 43 minutes, and I still sometimes win my age group "Old Farts Over 50." My wife Baiba and I have climbed 2 of the world's highest mountains, Kilimanjaro in Africa and Aconcagua in South America, before concluding that mountain climbing wasn't our sport. And we've been together for over 35 years, a success in itself these days – and maybe a record in Hollywood.

When it comes to money, I was never really interested in it or motivated by it, and I don't like to talk about it. But, like it or not, money is one indicator of success. So I guess I have to stand up and confess that I'm a... a... a... millionaire. Whew! Glad that's over.

The bottom line: I don't just talk about success, I've achieved it in a number of ways. But just being successful doesn't make me an expert on the subject. What gives me the real credentials to write this book is the decade I spent asking hundreds of great people what helped them succeed, then analyzing every word they said. So I still may not look like a successful guy, but I can sure tell you what really leads to success – and it's the *8 To Be Great*.

ABOUT **SPIKE**

You may be wondering about this little character named Spike. He started by accident when I drew him on a sign and gave him spiky hair. Then before I knew it the little creep took over the book. Spike represents all the ordinary people who reach extraordinary success. I made the character very simple so anybody can relate, regardless of gender, nationality, or race.

[Editor's note: The real reason he made Spike so simple is, even after spending years at art college, the guy still can't draw.]

8
TO BE
GREAT

1. **PASSION**

2. **WORK**

3. **FOCUS**

4. **PUSH**

5. **IDEAS**

6. **IMPROVE**

7. **SERVE**

8. **PERSIST**

1. PASSION

Great people follow their PASSION. They love what they do. Passion is a good starting point, because if you love it you're energized, and you'll automatically do all the other things that lead to success. It can take a long time to find your true passion, so if you haven't found it just keep looking. What if you're in a job you don't love? Just follow your real passion on the side. And make sure you follow your heart not your wallet. Go for the zing – not the ka-ching. The money will come anyway.

PASSION IS THE STARTING POINT

There are 8-Traits that lead to greatness in any field. They're all important but I put PASSION at the top of the list, because if you love what you do it will be so much easier to embrace the other traits.

When I ask great people what helped them succeed, the first word out of their mouths is often "love" or "passion." When **Russell Crowe** told me what led to his Academy Award for Best Actor he used both words: "The bottom line is I love the actual job of acting. I have a great passion for it. I love telling stories, so it's very simple for me to do my job."

Dave Lavery, the NASA whiz who sends robots to Mars, said to me, "Passion is almost an insufficient description of the way I felt. I discovered something I really loved, the thing that turned me on and got me excited. It made me want to get up and go to work every morning, and not want to go to bed at night."

Many people who grew up poor say it was passion that pushed them to the success they have today. **Graham Hawkes** told me he "grew up on the wrong side of everything." But passion took him from "living in a derelict cottage with no money" to designing a revolutionary ocean deep-diving system, founding 5 technology companies, and holding the world record for the deepest solo ocean dive. Graham says, "People around me tell me I'm just totally passionate and driven about what I do. I think it's normal."

Sometimes passion is mistaken for ambition. Famous real estate developer **Donald Trump** seems to be a very ambitious guy, but he says, "I'm not ambitious. I just love what I'm doing, and if you love what you do, you do a lot of stuff. And then people say, 'Oh, you're ambitious.'"

Whether it's the boardroom or the classroom, passion makes all the difference in any field. **Brian Little**, voted by students as the most popular professor at Harvard, says, "My personal project is teaching with a passion, and I'll do whatever I have to do to bring that project to fruition." Hey, I wanna be in that guy's class!

It's amazing what you can do when you love what you do. Passion has enabled **Aimee Mullins** to set running records, even though she's missing 2 essential limbs for running – legs. They were amputated below the knee when she was a child. But with the help of artificial legs and real passion, she set a number of world records at the Paralympics. She's well-named since "Aimee" comes from the French word for "love" and it's a big reason for her success on the track and in life. No wonder she says, "If it's your passion then inevitably you'll succeed."

> **I care passionately about the things that I do. I really want to do them. I don't know where it came from, but I'd recommend it.**
> *Jennifer Mather* renowned animal behaviorist

> **The only way to be truly satisfied is to do what you believe is great work. And the only way to do great work is to love what you do.**
> *Steve Jobs* CEO, Apple

GREAT PEOPLE IN ALL FIELDS LOVE WHAT THEY DO

Passion is a big key to success. And if you don't believe me, look at all the great people here who say they love what they do. The point is, no matter what the field, no matter what the job title, the people who really succeed absolutely love their work. The quotes speak for themselves.

BUSINESS

The fountain of youth is to love your work. I have a passion for what I do.

Sumner Redstone chairman, Viacom

DESIGN

I think there has to be a big passion in fashion.

Alexander McQueen fashion designer

FINANCE

I love the ability to create a capital structure that is appropriate for a company.

Henry Kravis cofounder KKR, world's biggest buyout firm

EDUCATION

I've spent my life doing what I love doing. At a very early age I found that I loved history.

Margaret MacMillan history professor, award-winning author

MUSIC

Nothing is more important than passion...Whatever you decide to do in life, just be passionate about it.

Jon Bon Jovi singer/songwriter

FOOD

I love what I do. I'm obsessed by it.

Charlie Trotter renowned chef

MEDICINE

I love dentistry. I can't imagine being anything else.

Izzy Novak dentist

PSYCHOLOGY

Passion is huge. I think being irrationally passionate is extremely healthy. Gravitate towards the things you love.

Sandra Yingling psychologist

SALES

I love it. I love getting up in the morning and going to work.

Elli Davis top real estate salesperson

SPORTS

I absolutely love it. I love hitting the golf ball.

Tiger Woods golf superstar

TECHNOLOGY

I found what I loved to do early in life. Woz and I started Apple in my parents' garage when I was 20.

Steve Jobs CEO Apple Inc.

WRITING

I love writing these books. I don't think anyone could enjoy reading them more than I enjoy writing them.

J.K. Rowling author, "Harry Potter" books

UNDERACHIEVERS
TURN INTO
SUPERACHIEVERS

ONCE THEY FIND THEIR PASSION

In today's world, kids are being pushed harder and harder to become overachievers, academically and in every other way. So I'm sitting here looking at my research and wondering why we want kids to overachieve, when so many successful people started out as underachievers. For example, who said this?

"…sitting in my room being a philosophical depressed guy, trying to figure out what I was doing with my life."

It was none other than **Bill Gates**. According to writer Janet Lowe: "In the sixth grade, Gates was underperforming in school, at war with his mother, and generally struggling with life. His parents decided to send him to a psychologist for counseling." Yeah, I can just hear people back then saying, "Boy, that Gates kid sure is a loser. He's never gonna go anywhere in life." But once Bill found his passion for software he took off – and became very well off.

And how about **Michael Eisner**? His sister was one of those grade "A" students and an excellent ice skater. Gee, compared to her, poor little Michael must have seemed like a kid going nowhere. He says he was interested in just existing and didn't have major goals. Funny how, once he found his passion in the entertainment industry, he became a renowned CEO of Disney.

Then there's **Ben Saunders**. Ben told me he has an old report card framed above his desk that reads: "Ben lacks sufficient impetus to achieve anything worthwhile." Interesting that once he found his passion for outdoor adventure, Ben could haul a 400-pound sled 800 miles and become the youngest person to ever ski solo to the North Pole. I'd say that takes a little "impetus."

UNDERACHIEVERS WHO BECAME SUPERACHIEVERS
ONCE THEY FOUND THEIR PASSION

Albert Einstein scientist	**Larry King** TV host
Bill Gates founder, Microsoft	**Issy Sharp** CEO, Four Seasons hotels
Frank Gehry architect	**Colin Powell** U.S. Secretary of State
John Grisham author	**Michael Eisner** CEO, Disney

Linda Keeler, general manager of Sony Pictures, says, "I got C's all through high school and I was a very lazy student. It wasn't until I got out of college that I applied myself and became very successful, because I found my passion. When you have a passion it makes a big difference." Yes, finding your passion is like slapping a turbocharger on a car engine. Same engine, yet far more powerful.

So it's okay for kids to get off to a slow start. If they're not Einstein at 8, don't panic. Even **Albert Einstein** wasn't Einstein at 8. Little Albert was the ultimate underachiever, who didn't speak until he was 3, stumbled his way through school, and worked for years as a low-level clerk in a patent office. But he followed his passion for physics, developed the Theory of Relativity, and became the world's greatest physicist. I'm sure Albert would say that how fast you reach success is all relative. Today's underachieving kids can turn into tomorrow's Einsteins, once they find their passion.

> **The energy comes from within**
> **if you love what you do.**
>
> *Keith Black* great neurosurgeon

THE **BIG PROBLEM** IS **FINDING** YOUR **PASSION**

STRIVERS KNOW WHAT THEY LOVE AND CAN HEAD STRAIGHT TOWARDS IT

SEEKERS DON'T KNOW WHAT THEY LOVE AND NEED TO DISCOVER IT

Passion is important to success, but the big problem is finding your passion. Oh sure, there's the kid who knows she wants to be a doctor or lawyer from the time she's 10. I call these people "Strivers" because they know what they love and can strive straight towards it. But I found another group of successful people, maybe a bigger group, I call "Seekers." They don't have a clue what their passion is and they need to seek it out. So, if you're sitting there thinking, "What's wrong with me? I don't know what I love," well, join the club. You're not alone.

In my research I found a lot of great Seekers who needed to discover their passion, including *Titanic* filmmaker **James Cameron**, Beatle **Paul McCartney**, homemaking guru **Martha Stewart**, Body Shop founder **Anita Roddick**, and evangelist **Billy Graham**. And once they found it they went on to great success. **Russell Campbell,** president of ABN AMRO Asset Management Canada, sums it up well when he says, "There's something in you that pushes you in a certain direction, and you just have to go with it. The hard part is figuring out what that is. I spent the first 30 years trying to figure out what that was."

Being a Seeker actually has some big advantages. You don't go down a predetermined path, so you're often the one who stumbles into uncharted waters and discovers new worlds. **Columbus** was seeking a passage to the East Indies and instead discovered the new world of America. Five-hundred years later **Jim Kimsey** didn't know where he wanted to go in life and his seeking led him to the new world of the Internet, and a different kind of America when he founded AOL, America Online.

Robert Ward, senior VP for design and planning at Universal Studios, said to me, "Many of us who have done neat things took a path that we never thought we would go down in the beginning. My background is painting and photography, and today I'm driving billion-dollar theme park projects for Universal Studios. So I like to think I paint with bulldozers." Robert added, "You don't always have to know what you want. Don't be afraid to say, 'I don't know what I want to do.' That will come in time."

But sometimes we are afraid to say that we don't know what we want to do, because we hear somebody brag, "My son's only 12 and he's going to be a lawyer." So we think it's better to be a Striver. Sure, Strivers may have less anxiety, since they know where they're going, but it's no better or worse; it's just one way. The other way is to be a Seeker who travels down uncertain roads, in search of unknown passions, and still arrives at the right destination – maybe a new, undiscovered destination. The truth is, you don't have to know where you're going in order to get there.

> **I don't know where I'm going, but I'm on my way.**
> *Carl Sandburg author, poet*

> **I didn't really know what I wanted to do in life. I was a load tester, a penitentiary service clerk, a mechanic. I know I like this better.**
> *Dan Aykroyd popular actor*

TO FIND PASSION
EXPLORE MANY PATHS

If we haven't found our passion, how exactly do we discover it? Well, unfortunately it's not going to drop into our laps as we sit at home with our feet up having a cold one. We've got to get out there and explore many paths. **T.K. Mattingly**, veteran astronaut and one of the real-life heroes of Apollo 13, said to me, "I've had a lot of experiences. I've been to places that provided opportunities to do things, and I just never said no. The more experiences, and the faster you get 'em, the better. They always pay off."

Robert Munsch told me he explored many paths to find his passion: "I studied to be a priest and that turned out to be a disaster. I tried working on a farm; they didn't like me. I worked on a boat; it sank. I tried a lot of different things that didn't work. But I didn't give up. I kept trying, and then I tried something that did work." I'd say it worked. With his passion for writing children's stories, Robert has sold over 40-million books in 20 countries. **Wade Davis** worked in a logging camp, then as a big game hunting guide, a park ranger, and a photographer. Then one day he knocked on the door of legendary plant explorer Richard Evans Schultes. "I said, 'I've saved up money and I want to go to South America with you to collect plants.' I didn't know anything about plants or South America and 2 weeks later I was in the Amazon." That knock on the door led Wade down the path to becoming a noted anthropologist, ethnobotanist, bestselling author, and *National Geographic Society* explorer-in-residence. Is that a cool title or what!

Exploring to find your passion doesn't mean you need to go all the way to the Amazon like Wade Davis. Another Davis, **Elli Davis**, told me she just went down the street. "I was a teacher, but I liked to read the real estate ads and I used to look at open houses on weekends. I was afraid to try real estate, but if I'd never tried it, I would never have known how good I could be at it. You must try it. Just do it." By just trying it, Elli found her real path to passion and rose to the top of the real estate profession.

So if you haven't found your passion keep exploring and looking. And it doesn't even require sight. **Erik Weihenmayer**, the first blind climber to summit Mt. Everest, says, "Follow your bliss, down dead-end alleys and to unseen places; it will lead you to a lifetime of happiness."

> **I needed to explore to find my passion. I started off as an engineer, then I went into management consulting, then product marketing, before I finally stumbled into venture capital.**
>
> ***Steve Jurvetson*** *renowned venture capitalist*

WHAT IF YOU'RE IN A JOB YOU DON'T LOVE?

If you're in a job you don't love, then just do what you love on the side. Remember, **Albert Einstein** worked as a patent clerk but his passion was physics. And he wrote 4 of his most important papers in his spare time! It's amazing what you can do if you love what you do.

FALLING
INTO YOUR
CALLING

They say you have to find your calling. But if it's a "calling," shouldn't it call you? I mean, your phone should ring and a deep, Darth Vader-type voice says, "You will become a brain surgeon!" and you go, "Gee, okay, thanks!" And you become a brain surgeon. But that's not how it works. Instead of a calling it should really be named a falling, because many successful people fall into their passion by accident.

Dawn Lepore told me she never planned to become the CIO in charge of all the information technology at Charles Schwab: "I fell into what I do, and I didn't know I loved it until I fell into it." Architect **Susan Ruptash** says, "I fell into architecture. I was sitting in the guidance counselor's office in high school, at the deadline to apply for university, without a clue what I should do. I started flipping through university calendars and stumbled on architecture. I thought, 'That looks interesting. I'll try it out for a year.' Here I am 20 years later. I discovered I loved it."

Optometrist **Jerry Hayes** says, "I stumbled into being an optometrist. I always wanted to be a dentist, so I went and talked to my local dentist, and he said, 'Why would you want to be a dentist? Become an optometrist instead.' I didn't even know what it was, but it turned out to be a better path because I didn't have enough hand dexterity, and the best dentists are good with their hands."

Sometimes we fall into our calling by falling out of something else. **Robert Full**, renowned professor of integrative biology, told me he fell into biology when he fell out of baseball: "I wanted to be a professional baseball player. I tried out for the Pittsburgh Pirates and didn't make it. Then on vacation at the beach I saw some weird animals and thought, 'Wouldn't it be great if I could somehow study the motion of these creatures?' And that's exactly what I'm doing."

Michael Furdyk fell into his calling when he turned his passion for computers into successful online companies and became a millionaire at the age of 17. He told me, "It was kind of an accident, which is the way I think these things usually happen. But you also have to be proactive about it." Yes, we can't just sit, waiting for our calling to call. It happens by getting off our butts, trying different jobs, going down different paths, then one day turning a corner and falling into what we're meant to do. As pioneer fabric designer **Jack Lenor Larson** says, "I fell in love with weaving, like falling into a trap, and I never wanted to get out."

If you haven't found something that makes you feel that way, keep looking. Be open to falling into your calling. And don't worry about hurting yourself. Just the opposite – it will make you feel absolutely wonderful!

> **I stumbled into personal computers and actually hit upon something that I was passionate about.**
> *Mitch Kapor founder, Lotus, designer of Lotus 1-2-3*

> **I fell into the health care industry by default when I got an admission into a pharmaceutical college, and it became an addiction for me.**
> *Aman Gupta CEO, Imprimis Life*

FOLLOW YOUR HEART

NOT YOUR WALLET

Hey, what about me?

GO FOR THE ZING

NOT THE KA-CHING

How do you find your passion? It's obvious — follow your heart. The problem is there's this other thing called a wallet we're often tempted to follow. Money is not easy to ignore, but the successful people I talked to said they've always been motivated by hot passion, not cold cash. They do it for the zing, not the ka-ching. And that even goes for people who deal with money. Wall Street investment banker **Lise Buyer** says, "Don't necessarily pick the job that has the highest salary attached, because that's not where you'll find your success. Pick the one that fires you up. What gets me out of bed in the morning is absolute love of the job."

Freeman Thomas, famous designer of cars such as the updated Beetle and Audi TT, told me he always followed his heart, not his wallet: "My first job at Porsche didn't pay very much, but it was my passion to go there. A lot of people at school went for the best offer and I went after my passion. I always let that be my guiding light and it's always done me well. The money comes eventually." GlaxoSmithKline Biologicals VP **Debbie Myers** had the same attitude when she was starting out: "I didn't really care about how much money I was making. That wasn't why I took a job. I took a job because I loved it, and the experience and opportunity it would give me. It ended up that I've been paid quite well."

Donovan and Green cofounder **Nancye Green** may have that color as her last name, but she says to forget about the green stuff and do what you love: "Forget how much money you're earning. Find a way to put food on the table, but feed your heart. I didn't care about having a lot of money. What I cared about was how excited I could get about what I was doing and the rest would follow – and it did."

I'm not saying money isn't in the minds of some successful people, especially those who come from poor backgrounds. But even they tell me that passion, not money, was the real motivator. Great graphic designer **David Carson** told me he gave up a good teaching salary to follow his passion for design: "I was never motivated by money. I worked for many years for little money. There were days when I couldn't get to the office because I didn't have money for gas. The goal was not money or fame. The goal was to do something I really enjoyed." And now David is both famous and very well off.

Science historian and author **James Burke** told me, "The least important things are fame or money. I mean, I'm perfectly happy to write books and articles and never come out of my room. It's not recognition. It isn't money, because I'm no good with money. I just like making the product."

So here's the acid test for knowing if you've found your passion: Would you do it for free? If you answer "Yes" then you've found it. If you answer "No" just keep looking. To quote **Jack Lenor Larson:** "You have one life, it better be the one you love."

> **The people who make it to the top – whether they're musicians or great chefs or corporate honchos...are the ones who'd be doing whatever it is that they love even if they weren't being paid.**
>
> *Quincy Jones legendary music composer, producer*

DO IT FOR LOVE

MONEY COMES ANYWAY

Recently I read a survey that said the life goal of most 18- to 25-year-olds is getting rich. When I read that I thought, "Gee, that's interesting. I've interviewed many millionaires and billionaires and they say their life goal was NOT to get rich. Their number-one priority was to do what they loved."

Bill Gates says money wasn't the motivation when he and **Paul Allen** started Microsoft. "Paul and I, we never thought that we would make much money out of the thing. We just loved writing software." And by loving it, they became two of the world's richest men. Basketball superstar **Michael Jordan** said, "I play the game because I love it. I just happen to get paid." A lot, I might add. Doing what he loved made Michael one of the highest paid sports figures ever.

Sometimes we think rich people go for the money, when in reality they go for the passion and stumble into the money as a result. Geneticist **Craig Venter** told me he's been described as an accidental millionaire: "I went into biology thinking I was going to be poor my whole life. There's nothing I've done because I was trying to get money. I've been pursuing my passion, and money has come along with it a few times. Don't pursue money."

I became a millionaire by following my heart, not my wallet. In fact, a number of times I walked away from money to do what I loved. Once was when I worked at Nortel Networks R&D labs. I had a dream job, working with terrific people, doing great projects, and was being paid a lot of money. But I wasn't doing what I really loved at the time, which was photography. So I thought I'd leave and start my own little photo company. My heart said, "Go for it." My wallet, and my friends, said, "Are you crazy? You can't walk away from the money. You're gonna starve."

Well, I listened to my heart, walked away from the money, and followed my passion. And sure, at first there wasn't much money, but it didn't matter since I was doing what I loved and having fun. And eventually the money came. I woke up one day and I was a millionaire. I learned it's true what they say: If you do it for love, the money comes anyway. (Note: To make a lot of money, we also need to serve others something they love. See the Serve chapter.)

So why does following your heart also fill up your wallet? Because if you do what you love you'll automatically work hard, focus, persist, and do all the other 8-Traits that lead to success and wealth. *The Simpsons* creator **Matt Groening**, who became very rich by following his passion, said to me, "I think that when you do what you love, you bring passion and enthusiasm to your job, so you are much more motivated to do a good job, which means you're more likely to be successful and to make more money."

So I'd say if you really want to get rich, put money at the bottom of your priority list, and passion at the top. Do what successful people do and follow your heart, not your wallet. In the end, your wallet will be happy you did.

> **Yes, I've made a great deal of dough from my fiction, but I never set a single word down on paper with the thought of being paid for it...I did it for the buzz. I did it for the pure joy of the thing.**
>
> ***Stephen King*** *bestselling novelist*

8 TO BE GREAT

1. **PASSION**

2. **WORK**

3. **FOCUS**

4. **PUSH**

5. **IDEAS**

6. **IMPROVE**

7. **SERVE**

8. **PERSIST**

2. WORK

Great people WORK very hard. Success doesn't come easily to anybody. It sometimes requires long hours and little sleep. But if you love what you do it doesn't seem like work, it seems like fun. So be a WorkaFrolic, not a workaholic. Develop a work ethic and trust that the hard work will pay off. It always does.

GREAT PEOPLE
WORK HARD

The second trait that makes people great is WORK. When I asked homemaking guru **Martha Stewart** what lead to her great success she said, "I'm a real hard worker. I work and work and work all the time. Never believe that others will do your work for you."

Yes, work is the basic entry fee for success, and all successful people work very hard, no matter what field they're in. Lawyer **Michael Frankfurt** said to me, "I had no big breakthroughs. I just kept going and worked hard. Even now, I'm the first to arrive in the morning." Author **Peter C. Newman** said, "I'm a very hard worker. I've always worked 2 jobs. I've written books from 4 in the morning, until about 9 or 10 o'clock, and then had a regular job."

Architect **Susan Ruptash** told me that when she was starting out, hard work gave her a head start: "In my first jobs I always tried to work harder than anybody else. I wanted to be the first person in the office in the morning and the last one to leave at night. The hard work led to opportunities, and that's probably a key to early success for anybody."

Like it or not, it's a competitive world and working hard can give you an edge. **Ted Turner** said the work edge helped him win the America's Cup world sailing championship: "You can't win races without working harder than the other guys." Ted also said, "Nothing ever came easy. My first eight years of sailing I didn't even win my club championship. But I just kept working and working and working. That's the secret of my success."

Great people think about their work even when they're not at work. **Leonard Susskind**, one of the world's top theoretical physicists, told me, "Thinking about physics I do 24 hours a day. I do it in the bathtub, I do it on the john, I do it while I'm taking a walk." When top independent analyst **François Parenteau** takes a walk up Wall Street, investing is on his mind: "Work is a big part of my life. I think about investment pretty much 24 hours a day, 7 days a week."

Work is also the key to Google's success, according to cofounder **Larry Page**: "We started working on Google 8 or 9 years ago when we were at Stanford. Since then we've worked on it really hard, 24 hours a day. You can't just have inspiration. It's maybe 10% inspiration and 90% perspiration."

Perspiration – sweat? Yech! Working hard can get pretty messy and smelly. But don't think of it that way. Think of it as the sweet smell of success.

> **All good things come from hard work and doing your best.**
> *Greg Zeschuk* "Game Developer of the Year"

> **Be committed to working very hard...I work like a demon, I really do.**
> *Sherry Cooper* economist and global strategist

> **You have to work like there's no tomorrow. If you're going to be successful at anything, the key thing is to work hard.**
> *Nez Hallett III* CEO, Smart Wireless

GREAT PEOPLE **AREN'T WORKAHOLICS**
THEY'RE
WORKA**FROLICS**

When doing the research for this book, I was listening to the radio while out for a run and I heard a program about the evils of work. It painted a picture of hard-working people as workaholics, slaving away with frowns on their faces, so addicted to work it ruins their health and life. I stopped in my tracks and thought, "Wait a minute, that's not right!" I've talked to hundreds of successful people, and yes they work hard, but they have smiles on their faces because they have tons of fun working.

Bell Mobility chairman **Bob Ferchat** said to me, "I was never a workaholic but I always worked 7 days a week because I was interested in what I was doing. It wasn't work, it was fun." I thought, "We need a new word to describe successful people who enjoy their work." Then it popped into my head: Successful people aren't workaholics – they're WorkaFrolics!

Chiat/Day advertising cofounder **Jay Chiat** is a WorkaFrolic. He says, "Absolutely have fun working. If you're not having fun, you're doing it for the wrong reasons." General Electric CEO **Jack Welch** is a WorkaFrolic: "Business is ideas and fun and excitement and celebrations, all those things." **Dave Lavery**, who's in charge of building the robots NASA sends to Mars, is a WorkaFrolic. He told me, "There are way too many sleepless nights. We work our fingers to the bone, but it doesn't seem like work. It's fun, it's what we want to do. We don't want to put things down in the evening and go home." **Sheldon Wiseman** runs an animation company, and he told me it's work that keeps him animated: "I work hard, but I've always had fun doing what I'm doing, and still do. I go to work every day and behave like a child and get paid for it."

WorkaFrolics have no dividing line between work and fun – it's both rolled into one. **Jimmy Pattison**, billionaire chairman of The Jim Pattison Group, says, "Business is my recreation. I'd rather go to a bunch of factories, meeting with our people, than go to Hawaii and stay on the beach, I can tell you that." And **Eve Ensler**, award-winning playwright of *The Vagina Monologues*, puts it this way: "I love to work. Work for me is pleasure, happiness. So I work 90% of the time, and I sleep the rest. I don't go on a vacation. That's not what gives me pleasure. Work gives me pleasure."

Everybody can find some type of work that's fun. Mathematics professor **Arthur Benjamin** told me he even has fun doing math: "My goal in life is to make more people love mathematics, and see that there's really a fun side to it that doesn't always get shown in school." Arthur is a true WorkaFrolic and he summed it all up when he said, "I feel happy doing work that I love. Before my father passed away, I asked him, 'Dad, what's the secret to a happy life?' and he said, without any hesitation, 'Find work that you really enjoy.'"

> **A true professional achieves success when you don't know what you're doing is work or play.**
> *Warren Beatty actor and producer*

> **I've always liked working. I think the biggest mistake I ever made was to retire. I didn't realize how much I really did love work. Now I'm back.**
> *Diane Bean VP business development, Manulife*

Successful people are WorkaFrolics – they have fun working. And by fun I don't mean it's always the "ha ha" kind of fun. Perhaps fulfilling is a better word to describe the work of a nurse or doctor taking care of patients, yet even in those circumstances there are moments of great joy. Other words people use to describe their work are enjoyable, gratifying, and engaging. But often they just say it's "fun!" Famous inventor **Thomas Edison** said, "I never did a day's work in my life – it was all fun."

Renowned architect **Jack Diamond** put it this way: "It's not hard work if you get a bang out of it. I do what I do because it's fun. I think that's the secret to success." **Darlene Lim**, post-doctoral fellow at NASA, says, "I love to have fun and work makes me feel good. I think hard work is probably 95% of the equation, but it doesn't seem difficult because it's enjoyable."

The business world may seem pretty serious but I found a lot of fun behind the scenes. Nortel VP **John Tyson** says, "If I can't laugh and I don't see that there's fun in it, I always ask: 'Why am I doing this?'" Even **Bill Gates** says he keeps doing his job because it's fun. And the fun helps propel people like Bill up to the top in the first place. I mean, if you have fun working you naturally work hard at it, so you do well, get promotions, and rise higher. That's why the top ranks of companies are full of WorkaFrolics. **Ian Craig**, president of Nortel Wireless Networks is one: "We always have a lot of fun. I say if you ain't havin' fun you ain't doin' it right." I watched Ian work and the way he kept thousands of people motivated wasn't with a whip, it was with his wit.

There's a strong link between fun, energy and success. It was fun that made **Wayne Gretzky** one of the world's great hockey players. He said, "The only way a kid is going to practice is if it's total fun for him...and it was for me." It was fun that helped make **Martin Short** a successful comedian: "My agenda has always been just to have fun because if you are having fun you can always find the energy you need that drives you." Yes, when people have fun, things get done. CNN founder **Ted Turner** says, "Struggling hard to achieve something is the most fun I get...People have the most fun when they're busting their ass."

Wait! Let's get realistic for a second. Are these WorkaFrolics having fun all the time? No. There's a lot of crap we all have to do that's no fun at all. The trick is to make sure you're having fun 80% of the time – and doing stuff that's not fun only 20% of the time. If it's the other way around, you're in the wrong job.

For many great people the fun doesn't wear off over time. Famous talk show host **Larry King** says he's having as much fun now as when he started out making $55 a week. And the fun is what helped propel Larry from 55 bucks to millions of bucks. Speaking of money, have you ever wondered why so many rich people don't retire? They're having too much fun! **Warren Buffett**, one of the world's richest men, could easily pack it in, but the fun still drives him. He says, "When I go to my office every morning, I feel like I'm going to the Sistine Chapel to paint." Do you feel that way when you go to work?

> **I played for fun for 9 straight years.**
> **We happened to win championships.**
>
> *Michael Jordan* basketball superstar

IT'S NOT EASY FOR ANYBODY

Success doesn't come easily to anybody, but the problem is we think it does. I remember driving home at 4 in the morning, after working non-stop for days, thinking, "Nobody else has to work this hard." But now, after interviewing more than 500 successful people, I know success never comes without a lot of effort. **Sherwin Nuland**, clinical professor of surgery at Yale, said to me, "It never came easy. It took a lot of very hard work. Some people don't understand. They seem to think that great things will happen just because they're wonderful."

Some occupations look easy. I mean you turn on the TV and entertainers don't seem to be working that hard. A comedian like **Chris Rock** stands up on stage and tells a few jokes. What's hard about that? But Chris says, "I wasn't the funniest guy growing up, but I was the guy who worked on being funny the hardest." I've directed films and I can tell you the best actors are also the hardest-working ones. Oscar-winning actor **Russell Crowe** said to me, "Films are a lot harder than people think. I've been training for this one for over 6 months and there's still another 2 months shooting to go. And I've been on this script for 7 years."

Writing seems like an easy job. No heavy lifting required. The words just flow for some people. Or that's what I believed as I struggled to put words on paper, thinking, "Why is it so hard for me?" Then I interviewed some great writers and they said it didn't come easy for them either. Bestselling author and explorer

Wade Davis told me, "Writing is never easy, and anyone who says writing is easy is either a bad writer or a liar."

Okay, how about retail? That's easy. Just open the door of your store and sit there waiting for customers to walk in. But when retail pioneer **J.C. Penney** was asked the key of his success, he said, "The answer is summed up in two words: hard work." Today nothing has changed, according to **Michael Budman**, cofounder of Roots clothing: "I have to work very hard. I love the business, but it takes a lot of time and energy and effort and creativity." Hey, what about opening a restaurant? People think that's an easy job. Well, **Drew Nieporent**, owner of Nobu and other top New York restaurants, says to think again: "It's never been easy. I've had to work very hard."

There has to be some easy job out there. Hey, I know! Now with the Internet and all the cool technology out there, maybe we can do "virtual" work instead of actual work. Let me ask **Jeff Bezos**, founder of amazon.com. I mean, he built his business on technology and the Internet. What's that? Jeff says, "I don't care what you want to do, you're gonna have to work hard." So much for virtual work. Guess we have to stick to the old-fashioned kind.

I have yet to find a person who achieved success without working hard. If you find one, let me know. I'll put them in the "Oddities of Nature" display in the museum, right next to the man they discovered who would actually ask people for directions when he was lost.

Easy street is a blind alley.
Wilson Mizner screenwriter

What happened to me is just an example of the American dream, of somebody busting their ass and working hard.
Bruce Willis popular actor

41

GREAT PEOPLE OFTEN **WORK LONG HOURS**

The other day I read an article that stated: "There is no correlation between success and hours worked." When I read that my blood boiled because it's simply not true. Based on my research, every successful person works long hours. Even after he was very rich, **Bill Gates** worked most nights until 10 o'clock and only took 15 days off in 7 years – and he probably spent them on his computer. **Oprah** says, "I would never see daylight. I'd come into work at 5:30 in the morning when it was dark and leave at 7:00 or 8:00 when it was dark. I went from garage to garage."

Once again, let me emphasize these folks are working those kinds of hours because they want to succeed at something and they love what they're doing. Cobalt Entertainment CEO **Steve Schklair** said to me, "I'll work 2 years straight, 7 days a week, 14-hour days, if I'm in love with a project." Yes, when something comes along you're passionate about it can take over your life and the hours shoot up. When filming *Star Wars*, **George Lucas** worked 16-hour days for 6 months with no days off. **David Cohen**, writer for *The Simpsons*, told me that when he was developing the *Futurama* TV series he "worked 100 days in a row, at one point, without a day off."

Ben Saunders told me his Arctic adventure meant skiing non-stop for months, hauling a 400 pound sled. Now that's work: "I skied for 72 days and only had 3 days off. You never really fully recover from one day to the next. So you wake up more and more tired." Yes, tired but happy, when the work paid off and Ben became the youngest person to ever ski solo to the North Pole. And Ben isn't alone in feeling tired. **Brendan Foster**, Olympic medalist and 3000m world record holder, once said, "All top international athletes wake up in the morning feeling tired and go to bed feeling very tired."

When we're starting out on the road to success, there's a big learning curve and that usually means extra hours. During his first year on the job as mayor of New York City, **Rudolph Giuliani** worked every single weekend, and in 8 years he only missed one day due to sickness. Renowned architect **William McDonough** says, "When I was starting out, I always worked long hours. I did 90-hour weeks when I was apprenticing." And musician **Ed Robertson** told me the early success of The Barenaked Ladies was due to tireless hard work: "We toured for 26 months straight and we earned the fan base one person at a time. We never took a break."

That's not to say successful people never take a break. They take a lot of breaks. And they often cruise along working basic 8-hour days until a passion or deadline comes along, and then the hours ramp up. Chiat/Day advertising cofounder **Jay Chiat** summed it up well for me when he said, "Be willing to work whatever it takes. It doesn't have to take long hours, but if it does take long hours you have to be willing to do it." I believe him, and I guess that's why I'm sitting here writing this at 3 o'clock in the morning.

> **I just worked my tail off, 12-hour and 14-hour days, for many years. No one said it was easy, but it was worth it.**
> *Kimberly King president, King & Assoc. Strategic Alliances*

> **I had to work as hard as I could 24 hours a day, to make it work, which is what I did. If you think you're gonna make it without work, fat chance.**
> *Ron Rice founder, Hawaiian Tropic*

FORGET TGIF
Thank God It's Friday
THINK
TGIW
Thank God I'm Working

If you ask a successful person what TGIF means, you just might get a blank stare. People who succeed in life really don't understand the "Thank God It's Friday" attitude. They're not the ones on a Friday afternoon lined up at the door like the start of the Indy 500, ready to rush out when the clock strikes 5. Instead of TGIF, successful people think TGIW – Thank God I'm Working. They're not afraid of hard work, they're afraid of no work. Famous graphic designer **David Carson** says, "It's not about the hours. I put in a lot of hours, but I'm enjoying it. I'm not watching the clock. I'm not waiting till 5 o'clock to go home."

Randall Larsen, founder of the Institute for Homeland Security, told me, "You can't be highly successful punching a time clock and saying, 'My 8 hours are up. I'm done for the day.'" And Dragon Systems CEO **Janet Baker** says, "A lot of these things are hard and take a lot of work. Saying you are only going to work so many hours on something sounds good, but life doesn't work that way."

Instead of a 9-to-5 attitude, successful people like Randall and Janet have a 5-to-9 attitude, so when others are leaving at 5, they stay and work until 9. As inventor **Thomas Edison** said, "I am glad the eight-hour day had not been invented when I was a young man. If my life had been made up of eight-hour days, I do not believe I could have accomplished a great deal."

And it's not just about accomplishment. Why wouldn't you work long hours if you love it and it's fun? That's why bestselling author **Stephen King** writes his novels every day of the year, including Christmas and his birthday: "For me, not working is the real work. When I'm writing, it's all the playground, and the worst three hours I ever spent there were still pretty damned good."

When you think about it, working a set number of hours a day is a new invention. Switzer Communications president **Jessica Switzer** says, "I grew up on a farm. You never stopped working, so I don't have a 9-to-5 mentality. It definitely instilled an around-the-clock work ethic in me." Hmmm… I wonder if that's why so many successful people grew up on farms? Working hard in the fields prepared them to work hard in any other field of endeavor.

Yes, great people work long hours and often get little sleep. (Can we start the sad violins playing please?) No wait! On second thought, we don't need to shed a tear for them. They're WorkaFrolics who love what they do and they're having fun. It's the people who yell, "TGIF" and rush off at 5 o'clock we should feel sorry for, because they're probably in the wrong job. As WorkCard chief strategist **Kathleen Lane** says, "Stress isn't working 15 hours at a job you like. Stress is working 15 minutes at a job you dislike."

> **It's not a 9-to-5 thing, where at 5 o'clock you just turn off your work and go home and kick back. It's something you love and it's with you all the time.**
>
> *Jaymie Matthews astrophysicist, mission scientist for the MOST space telescope*

WORK TOPS TALENT

Sometimes, when you're busting your buns, you can't help thinking, "If I'd just been born with more talent I wouldn't have to work so hard." Well, it might reassure you to know that what really makes people great is work, not talent. Professor **Michael Howe** and his colleagues at Exeter University examined outstanding performances in many areas and couldn't find anyone who reached the highest levels of achievement without thousands of hours of work and practice, whether in music, mathematics, chess, or sports.

Look at child prodigy **Mozart**. Everybody said the kid had talent, but he still had to work 12-hour days for over a decade in order to produce his first acknowledged masterpiece. **Michelangelo** produced some of the world's great art, yet he gave work, not talent, the credit for his genius: "If people knew how hard I worked to get my mastery, it wouldn't seem so wonderful after all." Today renowned artist **Ken Danby** says the same thing: "When people say to me, 'Oh, it must be so wonderful to have a God-given talent,' I say, 'That's a lot of crap.' Artists are disciplined. It's not a case of waiting for inspiration. You've gotta work."

I watched "America's Best Math Whiz" **Arthur Benjamin** stand on stage and have the audience shout out 3-digit numbers. Then he would cube the numbers in his head faster than the audience could do it with their calculators. When I asked him about his great talent he said, "I think numbers and I have always gotten along. But my talent, I'm sure, is just the matter of the time and hours I've put into it. To get good at anything really requires practice."

Some people who seem talented early in life end up not going very far. They figure their talent will carry them through, so they don't put in the work necessary for success. That's what happened to **Michael Jordan**. When he started playing varsity basketball he slacked off so much the coach cut him from the team. That little wake-up call made Michael realize he couldn't rely on talent alone and soon he became one of the hardest-working players. He even bullied the other players if they weren't putting in enough effort. (There's nothing worse than a reformed slacker.)

We overvalue talent and undervalue work because we don't see all the effort behind the scenes. We see the "talented" dancer's 15 minutes of fame, not the 15 years of work that went into it. We see the "talented" gymnast's perfect score of 10, not the 10 years of struggle to get there. We see the 200-page book, not the 20,000 hours the "talented" writer spent sweating over it.

The **Shakespeares**, **Picassos**, and **Einsteins** of the world might have had a spark to begin with, but it was work that turned the spark into a fire. So whether you have a natural gift of talent or not, there's an even greater gift you can give yourself, and that's the ability to work hard.

> **People would say to me, "You're so lucky to be talented," and I was always puzzled by that because every single drawing was a struggle for me. I spent a lot of time learning to draw.**
> *Robin Budd* animation film director

> **Everyone has some talent. Hard work is the real weapon in life.**
> *Martin Brodeur* top hockey goaltender

I WANTED A HORSE AND ALL I GOT WAS A

WORK ETHIC

When I was a kid I desperately wanted a horse. I was gonna be a cowboy, so a horse was a basic requirement for the job. I mean, galloping around on a broomstick just didn't cut it. I begged Dad for a horse, but he never gave in. Instead, he gave me something that turned out to be much better – a work ethic. Dad was a WorkaFrolic who always worked a lot and enjoyed it. By watching him, I picked up that same work ethic and it helped me succeed.

I've discovered that a strong work ethic is a common trait among successful people in all fields. **Silken Laumann** says it helped her become a world champion rower: "I think what my dad gave me at a young age was an appreciation for hard work leading to results." **Issy Sharp**, founder of Four Seasons Hotels, said to me, "I grew up in a household that gave us a work ethic. I never thought of work as being hard." Nurse **Janell Jacobs** told me a work ethic helps deliver better health care: "A work ethic not only affects you, it affects the people you work with. In my line of work, it affects the care of patients. If somebody doesn't do their job, it affects a patient's well-being."

I know this is hard to believe, but even great rock stars have a strong work ethic. I've seen many **Rolling Stones** concerts and I can tell you that **Gene Simmons** of **Kiss** is right when he says about the Stones: "They've maintained the work ethic of a brand-new band. They go out there every night and they deliver."

How do you pick up a work ethic? By hanging around people who have one, and often that means parents. **Anita Roddick**, founder of the Body Shop, says, "I was brought up in a large Italian immigrant family with a work ethic...we worked every weekend, every evening, and every holiday in the café." Architect **William McDonough's** family also had a strong work ethic, which meant William had to work more than many other kids: "We had to pay our own way through school. I had 2 paper routes, and shined shoes, and worked every vacation." *Time Magazine* called William "a hero for the planet" so I'd say his work ethic paid off for him, as well as the world.

But what if you were born into a family without a work ethic? Well, just find a WorkaFrolic who likes to work – a mentor, boss, coach, or role model – and hang out with them. In no time, their work ethic will rub off on you. The trick is to be with people who have fun at work, not those who make fun of work.

In hindsight, a work ethic is the best gift dad ever gave me (although at the time I would have preferred the horse). But material things and money soon disappear. Instead, give kids a strong work ethic and it will carry them into the sunset, and on to success.

> **I come from a family that has an incredible work ethic...When I was 12, I said to my dad, "When do I get my first allowance?" He said, "When you get a job." So I got a job the following day at a bicycle store, and became their number one salesperson.**
> *Kenneth Tuchman founder, TeleTech*

> **The first qualification for success in my view is a strong work ethic.**
> *Henry Ford II president of Ford*

TRUST
THAT
HARD
WORK
WILL
PAY
OFF

Sometimes, when you're putting a lot of effort and hours into something, you wonder if it will ever pay off. I remember times when I was working all night, and in the back of my mind I'd be thinking, "Is it worth it? Maybe this is all for nothing, so why bother?" Usually I'd just shove those doubts aside and keep going. Now, in hindsight, I'm glad I did because eventually the work did pay off, and I learned to trust that it always would. As basketball superstar **Michael Jordan** once said, "I've always believed that if you put in the work, the results will come."

Jerry Hayes, optometrist and founder of Hayes Marketing, says, "Keep it in your mind: I can make this work because I'm gonna work hard! The self-confidence that you can outwork the other guy will carry you through a lot." It carried **Wayne Schuurman**, president of Audio Advisor, through a lot of hot water when his company was in financial trouble. He says, "I had to come up with a genius way of saving the business. And my genius way of saving everything was to get up in the morning and go to work. I had friends that this happened to, and they stopped working and goofed off. But I went to work every day and worked as hard as I could. I didn't stop. I just kept pushing. And eventually it worked out."

Trusting work is like trusting the wind. When I first started windsurfing, if there was a really strong wind, I'd stand upright on the board and try to pull the sail around, but the wind would catch it and I'd become a human projectile, catapulted across the board into the water. After watching me wipe out about 200 times, a guy who actually knew what he was doing came over and said, "When it's really blowing, the way to get going is to fall backwards and then, just before you hit the water, pull the sail around into the wind. It takes a leap of faith because you think you'll land in the water, but you have to trust that the wind will hold you up."

I tried it and, like magic, it worked. From that moment on I remembered "trust the wind." So when it was blowing hard, I'd just fall backwards, the wind would catch the sail, and it would hold me up. It's the same when life is blowing hard and you're putting in lots of hours, and you're not sure if it's really getting you anywhere. At times like that, just fall into work, keep going, and trust that the effort will hold you up and pay off – because in the end it will. Great college football coach **Lou Holtz** once said, "No one has ever drowned in sweat." I'd go a step further and say: "Sweat is like a river that carries you along and keeps you swimming towards success."

> **You must have faith that your work ethic and your discipline have prepared you to be successful.**
> *Rick Pitino renowned basketball coach*

> **Know that hard work is going to pay off. It may not pay off today, but the longer you stick with something the more it pays off. You just have to put time in on the treadmill and trust that it is going to make a difference.**
> *Kate Laidley vice president, JN4D*

8
TO BE
GREAT

1. **PASSION**

2. **WORK**

3. **FOCUS**

4. **PUSH**

5. **IDEAS**

6. **IMPROVE**

7. **SERVE**

8. **PERSIST**

3. FOCUS

Great people FOCUS. We can start by thinking wide, but success requires narrowing down and focusing all our energy on one thing. Remember, successful people aren't great at everything, they're only great at one thing. So have a long-term, single-minded focus that makes you an expert at something. In the short-term, be able to block out distractions, put your head down and CONCENTRATE.

The third trait that makes people great is FOCUS. Renowned filmmaker **Norman Jewison** said to me, "I think it all has to do with committing yourself and focusing yourself to one thing. I believe to do one thing well brings not only satisfaction, it also brings a kind of confidence. We become very confident when we know we can do one thing well."

Professor of mathematics **Arthur Benjamin** said, "I think every successful person spends an intense amount of time focused on one activity they really love." And Arthur's intense focus on math turned him into "America's Best Math Whiz." When I talked to **Dean Kamen**, instead of asking what leads to success, I asked, "What leads to failure?" And the first thing he said was, "To be a failure, don't focus." Dean's focus on technology solutions for health problems led him to over 150 patents and the invention of some very cool devices, like the first portable insulin pump, the heart stent, and the Segway human transporter.

Focus is all about specializing in something and becoming an expert. Psychiatrist and Stanford professor **Ken Woodrow** says, "You do have to be an expert in some area in order to bring something to the party and give back in a meaningful way." **Joseph MacInnis**, a doctor who became an expert on how the human body functions best underwater, told me "You need to have a specialty, which is the platform upon which you stand very firmly. In my case, I was a physician, but I specialized in physiology and divers working at extreme depths." That focus helped Joe become the first person to dive under the North Pole, and also be among the first to explore the wreck of the Titanic.

Developing an expertise means we can't just do something for a week, then fly off and do something else. Becoming great at anything – a career, a goal, a project – means staying focused on that one thing for months, years, or even decades. It took downhill skier **Picabo Street** 22 years of focus to become a gold medalist in the Olympics. **Louis Monier** told me it took intense focus for 5 years to develop Alta Vista, one of the first good search engines for the web. Grammy award-winning vibraphonist **Gary Burton** said it's all about hanging in there: "After a number of years of focus you reach a point of proficiency. For me, it was about 20 years, working at it pretty intently."

The focus and expertise of great people can often be summed up in less than 5 words. Can you describe your focus in less than 5 words?

Martin Luther King Jr. - Civil rights focus
Frank Gehry - Sculptural architecture focus
Michael Jordan - Basketball dunking focus
Martha Stewart - Homemaking focus
Albert Einstein - Relativity focus
Bill Gates - PC software focus

Focus is absolutely critical. Many people work really hard, but they're not focused. They're flying around trying to do too many things, and the work they're doing becomes diluted.
Susan Ruptash *architect, principal, Quadrangle*

I followed my dream and I just stayed focused. And I didn't give up. Focus.
Peter Max *renowned pop artist*

GO WIDE THEN FOCUS

Success means narrowing down and focusing on one thing, not being scattered all over the map. But wait! (Here comes the disclaimer.) Don't focus too soon. At the beginning of anything – a career, a goal, a project – we need to do the opposite of focus. We need to start by thinking wide.

That's why they invented schools, so we get exposed to many different subjects and discover what turns us on. And, believe it or not, all those seemingly useless subjects come back later to help us with in the one thing we focus on. **Bob Rogers**, founder of BRC Imagination Arts, says, "In school, some people ask, 'What does this course have to do with anything?' But eventually it all relates. It's only in retrospect that you find out every single course was useful."

Adam Bly, founder of *SEED* science magazine, says that thinking wide is often what plants the seeds for our future focus: "At first you go wide and let yourself wander a little bit to figure out the best way of getting there but, at the end of the day, it requires long-term focus to get there." Renowned medical geneticist **Josef Penninger** told me, "You need to think broadly, because you have to take pieces from here and there and fit them together into a specialty – and then it clicks." It clicked for Josef when he focused on curing osteoporosis and uncovered the master gene that causes it.

Studying to be a doctor requires intense focus, but **Sherwin Nuland**, a famous clinical professor of surgery at Yale, told me he started out by thinking wide: "I didn't focus early in my career. I thought broadly. You want to learn everything you can get your hands on. By the time I went to medical school, I'd learned about literature and history, and you're much better when you focus, because you bring all of these wide things to the table."

Google cofounder **Larry Page** said to me, "You should focus on one important goal. It takes a long time to do these things and you need to be pretty single-minded. But you also need to really understand all the different parts. At Stanford, we built the whole search engine so we had to understand all the parts, we had to interact with the world, and we had to innovate in different areas like business, not just computer science, to make our system work."

Yes, thinking wide is important at times, but if we do it for too long our energy becomes dispersed in too many different directions. We become dabblers in many things and masters of none. So, at some point, we need to shift gears, narrow down, and focus in on one area. As **Don Norman**, author of *The Way Things Work*, says, "You have to think broadly in the beginning, but you're never going to finish anything unless you focus."

When you focus the sun's rays through a magnifying glass, it can generate enough energy to create a fire. So use the same principle in your own life. Intensely focus all your energy on one thing, and it will help fire up your own success.

> **You explore the landscape and then you focus deeply in one area. You survey and then you drill down.**
> *Kim Rossmo* renowned criminologist

> **When I'm trying to plan, I think very broad. But when I'm trying to accomplish something, I'm very focused.**
> *Deborah McGuinness* senior research scientist, Stanford

If there's one word that sums up why I wasn't living up to my full potential at one point in my life, it would be "dabble." I mean, after spending 10 years in the work force I was still dabbling in many different areas: research, design, project management, presentations, writing, and advertising photography. On the personal front, I was dabbling in sailing, rowing, and running, plus taking music, cooking, and French classes. Whew! Being scattered all over the map meant I never stopped in any one place long enough to become really good at something. And let's face it, there's not much demand for professional dabblers. When you look in the classified ads for a job you don't see ones like this:

Senior Dabbler required for growing midtown firm. Three years minimum experience, preferably accumulated only 20 minutes at a time. Candidate must have only superficial knowledge. Those with any real expertise need not apply. Preference will be given to those with a short attention span and an MDA – Must Dabble Always.

If you look at successful people, you'll find they're not great at a lot of things – they're only great at one thing. **Quincy Jones** can't even drive a car, or a nail. He says, "I couldn't drive a nail in the wall if my life depended on it." But he focuses on making beautiful music and that's all that matters. (For more examples see the Improve chapter – Focus On Your Strengths.)

I realized that to get anywhere I had to focus and become an expert at something. I loved photography, but it was always a sideline. Now it was time to focus on it and see how far I could take it. So I stopped dabbling at the big corporation, started my own company, and focused all my energy on photography. The personal dabbling in music, French, and cooking classes also had to go. (No big loss. My real strength was eating, not cooking.) The focus paid off and I finally started to get somewhere. I became a successful advertising photographer, my work appeared in international magazines, and I even shot a cover for *Playboy*. But, as I said in the introduction, only once. My wife reminded me of that old Zen saying: "He who shoots bunnies could also get shot."

Over time, my passions and focus morphed from photography to research, to marketing, video production, and writing. But, at any one time, I focused 100% on only one thing. No dabbling. And each time the intense focus paid off in terms of quality, satisfaction, awards – oh, and I almost forgot – money. The bottom line is, if you really want to reach your potential, FOCUS.

> **If you want to be a great software company, you have to be only a software company – you can't dabble in other things.**
> *Bill Gates chairman, Microsoft*

> **To do a good job at something you've got to concentrate in one area, not be a jack-of-all-trades.**
> *Ted Turner broadcasting and entertainment tycoon*

We have a million things on our minds every day. But we can't succeed at a million things. It's hard enough to succeed at just one thing. That's why it helps to develop a single-minded focus. As philanthropist **John D. Rockefeller Jr.** once said, "Singleness of purpose is one of the chief essentials for success in life...."

A single-minded focus enabled **Cathy Rigby** to take home Olympic gold in gymnastics. She said, "I couldn't think of anything else but winning a gold medal." Scientist **Eva Vertes** was only 15 when her single-minded pursuit to wipe out Alzheimer's disease led her to a major discovery and possible cure. She told me, "Focus and dedication are important. You have to devote your whole life to one thing for a while. I devoted my life to getting started in Alzheimer's. Getting started is the hardest part, and if you don't have focus and determination you'll just go off on tangents."

A single-minded focus enabled astrophysicists working on the MOST space telescope project to do something nobody else could do – build a suitcase-sized satellite costing $10 million, compared to the $2-billion cost of the huge Hubble space telescope. **Jaymie Matthews**, astrophysicist and mission scientist for the MOST space telescope, told me, "Focus is the key word for our success.

We pulled this off on such a tight budget and short time line because we did one thing exceptionally well. We didn't try to make the Swiss Army knife of telescopes that did a lot of things."

Lawyer **Susan Grode** works with successful people in many fields and she said to me, "One of the things I've observed among many of my clients is how single-minded they are in pursuit of a goal. It can be constructing a new city, a new sculpture, their next joke, but they're absolutely single-minded in that pursuit. And they refuse to let the world deter that focus." TeleTech founder **Kenneth Tuchman** is a good example of that. He says, "I have this vision that is constantly evolving in my head. I go to sleep thinking about it, and wake up thinking about it, and have the shower beating me on the back while I am thinking about it."

Just a word of caution: Don't confuse single-minded with narrow-minded. Narrow-minded means refusing to accept new information, but successful people are like sponges, always absorbing new stuff from many different areas, because it gives them new perspectives they can apply to their single-minded pursuit. So even though you're focused on one thing, keep lifting up your head, looking around at the world, and absorbing something new. Take it all in, then switch gears and get back to the single-minded focus that will really help you succeed.

> **I have a singular focus. I've kind of become obsessed with work and obsessed with the product.**
> *Rick Mercer* political satirist and comedian

> **You must be single-minded. Drive for the one thing on which you have decided.**
> *George Patton* famous army general

> **I think you have to be very single-minded to stay focused enough to really break through whatever you're doing. I was single-minded to the point of being obsessive.**
> *Thomas Dolby* renowned musician

GREAT COMPANIES

Great people focus and so do great companies. When **Bill Gates** started Microsoft he didn't try to do everything under the sun. He focused on one thing and one thing only, saying, "Microsoft is designed to write great software. We are not designed to be good at other things. We only know how to hire, how to manage, and how to globalize software products."

Domino's Pizza thrived because they focused on pizza, and within that they focused on speed of delivery. When founder **Tom Monaghan** was asked the key to his success, he said, "A fanatical focus on doing one thing well." **Warren Buffett** became the world's most successful investor by focusing. He said, "I can't be involved in 50 or 75 things. That's a Noah's Ark way of investing – you end up with a zoo that way. I like to put meaningful amounts of money in a few things."

In the mobile email market, some companies tried to make a device that did everything, but Research In Motion focused on doing only one thing really well – always-on email that automatically comes to your BlackBerry. That focus gained them an early lead in the market, which is why **Jim Balsillie**, co-CEO of RIM, says, "Focus. The more experienced I get, the more I realize that great focus is an excellent competitive strategy."

Sleep Country founder **Gord Lownds** told me the big challenge is maintaining your focus: "My thinking has always been fairly broad, but I've learned that in business you do need to focus. I think the biggest mistake that people make is that they tend to lose their focus on a commodity or what the real business is, and they let their attention drift." Many companies drift off focus because they succeed at one thing, like widgets, so they think, "Why not try food products or investing?" But those diversions often fail because they lack the intense amount of focus needed to succeed. Research In Motion founder **Mike Lazaridis** cautions that when you're successful, instead of losing focus you actually need to focus deeper. And that approach kept BlackBerry at the head of the wireless email pack.

Bill Tatham maintained his focus. He started Janna Systems, a customer relationship software business, in his basement and focused on serving a small niche of financial services firms. As the company became more successful, Bill refused to diversify. He says, "The key was our maniacal focus. You have to learn to say no to opportunities that don't fit your strategy." Bill's focus paid off big-time when he sold the little business he started in his basement for over a billion dollars. The moral of the story is, if you want your business to go from basement to billions – FOCUS.

> **My focus is only on the health industry.
> I do nothing else.**
>
> *Anula Jayasuriya* venture capitalist

> **What it takes to make a company successful
> is laser-like focus on just one thing.**
>
> *Bill Gross* chairman, idealab

DEVELOP THE ABILITY TO CONCENTRATE

Focus actually has 2 parts: FOCUS and CONCENTRATION. We tend to use these words interchangeably and I always wondered, "What's the difference?" So I looked in the dictionary and it said the definition of focus is "to concentrate" and the definition of concentrate is "to focus." Whew, glad they cleared that up! But having focused, or concentrated, on the subject for years, here's how I see it: Focus is more long-term, like focusing on a career or a big goal. Concentration is more short-term such as concentrating on getting something done right now. Both focus and concentration mean zeroing in on one thing and blocking everything else out.

The ability to concentrate helped **Jeong Kim** develop a successful technology company and sell it for $500 million to Lucent. He said, "I can just work day and night and maintain the concentration. And I've never met anybody who can work as long and reach the same level of concentration without getting burned out."

The ability to concentrate helped **Tiger Woods** become the world's greatest golfer. He says that when you're about to hit that ball, it has to be the only thing you're thinking about, the only thing that matters at that point in time and "everything else is shunned away and put aside. You focus on what you want to accomplish right here and now." And concentration doesn't necessarily mean being alone in a quiet place. Tiger's ability to concentrate really pays off when he's inundated by noisy fans yelling "so loud that your eardrums are ringing by the time you tee off." He just blocks it all out and performs. And Tiger's great ability to concentrate on where he wants that little white ball to go, has taken him to where he wants to go.

Developing the ability to concentrate is all about training and practice. Olympic gold medal hurdler **Edwin Moses** says, "Concentration is why some athletes are better than others. You develop that concentration in training. You can't be lackluster in training and concentrate in a meet." **Lindsay Sharp**, who heads up the National Museum of Science and Industry in London, told me, "It's very hard to concentrate, so you have to practice a lot and it gets built up like any muscle. I wasn't taught. I learned how to study in the middle of an airport. So now if I'm focused on reading or writing and there's a fire siren going, I don't even hear it."

Being able to snap into concentration mode will help you no matter what you are doing, whether it's finishing a project, writing a letter, painting a wall, doing a term paper, working on a court case, or winning a race. As track and field great **Babe Didrikson Zaharias** once said, "My formula for success is simple: Practice and concentration – then more practice and more concentration."

> **I have a ferocious ability to concentrate. I can say, "I am going to do this," and close the rest of the world off. And I think that matters an awful lot in any job.**
> *Jennifer Mather* renowned animal behaviorist

> **The secret of my success? Concentration.**
> *Chris Evert* tennis legend

TO CONCENTRATE
ELIMINATE

Concentration is important, but it's hard to concentrate if we're constantly distracted. What's a distraction? Anything that's either fun or noisy. This includes TV, music, movies, video games, parties, and sports (with the exception of lawn bowling). Things that are not fun or noisy are rarely distracting. I mean, when was the last time you were distracted by broccoli or a librarian? But now with cell phones, email, web-surfing, and chat lines, it's a wonder we can concentrate for more than a nanosecond before something rings, beeps, or warbles. And every day, scientists are busy inventing new distractions (although it's not easy because they're constantly getting distracted).

Successful people need concentration time, so they find ways to eliminate those distractions. TV has grown into a huge, widescreen, stereo-sound, gazillion channel distraction, so renowned venture capitalist **Steve Jurvetson** eliminated it: "You can't do it all, so I actually cut out a lot of extraneous things. I haven't watched television for 18 years. I don't miss it." Great novelist **Stephen King** says to be a writer, "If possible, there should be no telephone in your writing room, certainly no TV or video games for you to fool around with. If there's a window, draw the curtains or pull down the shades unless it looks out at a blank wall. For any writer, but for the beginning writer in particular, it's wise to eliminate every possible distraction."

Warren Buffett became one of the world's richest men by living in a state of no distraction – Nebraska. He says, "I used to feel, when I worked back in New York, that there were more stimuli just hitting me all the time...It's much easier to think here." Hmmm... I wonder if fewer distractions could be one reason that small towns produce so many successful people? I'm no longer surprised when a successful person tells me they grew up in East Cupcake or another out-of-the-way place. **Elinor MacKinnon**, the CIO in charge of information technology at Blue Shield, says, "I grew up in a rural environment, and I think it helped form my thinking processes because there's not a lot of distractions. You can spend a lot of time inside your own mind thinking about things."

People often go to a distraction-free place if they need to concentrate. When **Wade Davis** was writing a book, he went to a cabin in the wilderness where he worked 14 hours a day for 7 months with no distractions, and came back with the bestselling *The Serpent and the Rainbow*. A cabin in the woods! Hey, maybe that's what I need. I mean there are so many distractions here in the city I'm having real trouble concentrating long enough to finish this section on concentration. I'm sure I'd get a lot more writing done in a cabin in the woods. I wonder if they get satellite TV?

> **You can surf the internet or watch TV and get distracted very easily. Writing means that you have to tune everything out and just focus on that.**
> *Meredith Bagby* CNN reporter, author

> **I find the most successful people are willing to forego many of the diversions that occur along the way, in order to stay true to their goal.**
> *Susan Grode* lawyer

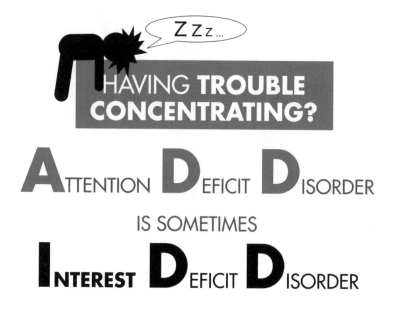

HAVING **TROUBLE** CONCENTRATING?

ATTENTION **D**EFICIT **D**ISORDER

IS SOMETIMES

INTEREST **D**EFICIT **D**ISORDER

What's the easiest way to concentrate on something? It's simple. Be interested in it. Of course, there will always be things we need to do that aren't the least bit interesting, and we need to learn to concentrate on those too. But if you can find things that interest you, it will be a lot easier to stay tuned in.

David Jensen, chief executive of Brooklands Executives Recruitment, says, "I can concentrate on things that interest me. But give me a task, whether it's academic or sporting or something that I'm not interested in, and I fail at it. So I tend to hone in on the things I find interesting." CAE president **John Caldwell** agrees: "A lot of people's success in business is more determined by their level of interest rather than their ability to do it. If you're not interested, it's hard to do it, no matter how important it is."

These days you hear a lot about kids with ADD – Attention Deficit Disorder. It can be a serious illness, but I think ADD is sometimes IDD – Interest Deficit Disorder. Some kids just aren't interested in the stuff they're told to concentrate on. But it's funny how they can concentrate like crazy on something they do find interesting, like an exciting video game or the latest trendy shoes. Maybe **Bill Gates** had IDD. He got poor grades in school subjects that didn't interest him and his parents even sent him to counseling. But once Bill found something that did spark his interest – computers and software – his ability to concentrate kicked in big-time.

I, too, suffered from IDD, since most school subjects didn't interest me, especially English, where we had to write essays on boring things I couldn't care less about. My attention wandered so much they had to send out search parties to find it. No wonder I ended up with a 66 in 12th grade English. Now fast forward to when I was out in the real world producing videos. I hired writers to develop scripts but I wasn't happy with the results, so one day I started writing scripts myself, without any training and purely out of interest. And suddenly I had no trouble concentrating. You couldn't tear me away from writing. I focused on it, got better, and even won an award for the best corporate video script in the world. So let's see... I went from getting a mark of 66 writing essays in high school, to a top award writing video scripts, and the only difference was interest – the magic ingredient that made it easy to concentrate.

The truth is we all find it hard to concentrate on some things and easy to concentrate on others, and a lot of it has to do with following your interests and doing what you love. Now, if I could only find a way to get interested in cleaning up the house...

> **Find things that you like a lot, so you're willing to focus on them. I don't focus on things I don't like.**
> *Nathan Myhrvold* chief technology officer, Microsoft

> **It's knowing your interests and working at those. I'm definitely not lazy, but I'm lazy about doing things that don't interest me.**
> *Cliff Read* award-winning product designer

8
TO BE
GREAT

1. **PASSION**

2. **WORK**

3. **FOCUS**

4. **PUSH**

5. **IDEAS**

6. **IMPROVE**

7. **SERVE**

8. **PERSIST**

4. PUSH

Great people PUSH themselves. They push through barriers like shyness and self-doubt. They push beyond what's expected. They push boundaries, push the envelope, push themselves to do the impossible. So just keep pushing yourself. And if you're having trouble, get a challenge, goal, deadline, competitor, or mother to push you.

PUSH
YOURSELF

The fourth trait that makes people great is PUSH. They just keep pushing themselves. Renowned marine scientist **David Gallo** said to me, "Push yourself. Man, that's huge. Always. Physically, mentally, you've gotta push, push, push."

Pushing himself has helped **William McDonough** become one of the world's great architects. He said, "When I'm working on a project, I may not know what the result will be, but I know that we're going to keep pushing until we all succeed." Pushing herself helped **Silken Laumann** become a world-champion rower: "As a rower, I'm average size and average weight. In order to beat some of the really big, strong, single scullers that I compete against, I need a little extra edge. And I think that extra edge, to a great extent, is the mental ability to push myself."

Chris Kilham has journeyed to remote parts of the world to learn about different herbs and how they can be used for healing. Chris says it's exciting but also scary: "I do push myself. I'm not some sort of Indiana Jones character who grew up in the wilds, so I do have to push myself to go to some of the environments that I go to and participate in some of the things that I do."

Oh, I should clarify that pushing yourself doesn't mean being pushy, like those people who are always pushing in front of you in line. (Don't you hate that?) I've interviewed a lot of great people and not one came across as pushy. **Steve Schklair**, CEO of Cobalt Entertainment, said to me, "I'm not a pushy kind of guy, but I push myself." Adventurer **Ben Saunders** said, "I'm not the driven, controlling type. I'm a pretty laid-back character and I kind of go with the flow. But I do push myself extremely hard, and I expect high things from myself."

The ability to push ourselves helps get us through the down times and all the stuff we don't want to do. Top real estate agent **Elli Davis** said, "Some days, I'm just in a bad mood. I don't want to call this person again and again and again. I just push myself." Legendary management consultant **Peter Drucker** summed it up by simply saying, "Push, push, push and you see results."

Successful people push themselves through shyness, doubt, and fear. They push boundaries. They push limits. They push beyond what's expected. It all comes down to pushing themselves in one way or another, and that's how they discover what they're really capable of. Virgin Group founder **Richard Branson** said to me, "I think whatever you're doing in life just push yourself to the limits. I like to push and see what I'm capable of, and I think people get more satisfaction out of life if they lead their life in that way." So just keep pushing yourself.

> **I've had to push myself, and had to stretch in ways that I didn't know I could possibly stretch.**
> *John Girard CEO, Clickability*

> **Push yourself. Try hard. You don't just sit and wait for life to happen to you.**
> *Leslie Westbrook marketing consultant*

> **I push myself, and I push my employees and partners and everybody else. I think it's important to push. If you push you get to a new level of ability.**
> *Wallace Eley president, Crossey Engineering*

PUSH THROUGH **SHYNESS**

Many successful people are shy but they keep pushing through it

One big internal barrier we need to keep pushing through is shyness. I'm constantly amazed at how many successful people are shy. TED conference chairman **Chris Anderson** doesn't seem the least bit shy when I see him on stage speaking to thousands of people, yet he told me, "I was shy as a kid, and I still am." **Elli Davis** said to me, "As a teenager, I was quite insecure, quite shy really. I kept everything inside." But Elli pushed through the shyness and became a top real estate agent.

The people we see on TV don't seem to be the least bit shy, but actor **Rip Torn** says many big-time actors and performers also have big-time shyness: "I think most actors are shy. I really do. The greatest actors can disappear." Top fashion model **Erin O'Connor** is shy: "I was a very, very tall, awkward girl in school. I am painfully shy." And you wouldn't think Miss Universe winner **Natalie Glebova** could ever be shy, but she was: "In high school I was shy because of my Russian background and accent. The other kids picked up on that and I was not accepted in a group. I didn't have many friends."

People may be shy in some situations, but not in others. Brooklands Executives CEO **David Jensen** says, "I was not shy. I was always very outgoing. But I'm not very good at walking into a crowd and networking with strangers. In that context, I'm shy. There's self-doubt and apprehension, and I don't want to force myself on people."

The good news is, based on the huge number of shy people out there who succeed, being shy doesn't have to stop you. As proof here are two shy guys who won the ultimate success indicator, the Nobel Prize. **James Watson** won it for finding the structure of DNA but he was so shy he couldn't find a date. James said to me, "I had one arranged date in college and it was a failure. I was shy with girls." So was Nobel Prize-winning physicist **Richard Feynman**, who writes, "I was not very good socially. I was so timid that when I had to take the mail out and walk past some seniors sitting on the steps with some girls, I was petrified: I didn't know how to walk past them!" Hey, I can relate!

Now comes the "but." Yes, these Nobel Prize winners started out shy, but over time they both pushed past it. Richard Feynman became known for the fascinating lectures he gave to large audiences, and James Watson said to me, "You can be shy, but with some people you shouldn't be shy. It's a weakness if you don't know other people."

The bottom line is you can be shy and still succeed. Many great people do. But like them, you also need to keep pushing yourself through the shyness. In the end, it's worth it. Like James and Richard, you might even win a really big prize.

> **I really admire people who can get in there and mingle and just work a crowd, but not me. I like people, but I'm shy.**
> *Ralph Famiglietta Emmy Award-winning art director*

> **I make my living talking to people. I've been in front of audiences of 1000 people. I just love it. But put me in a room full of strangers at a cocktail party and I'm terrified. I can't make small talk.**
> *Steven Schwartz author, "How To Make Hot Cold Calls"*

PUSH THROUGH SHYNESS

BUT KEEP THE GOOD THINGS YOU GET FROM BEING SHY

SHY PEOPLE OFTEN SPEND MORE TIME

READING LEARNING FOCUSING
LISTENING OBSERVING IMAGINING

So I got to thinking: If there are countless numbers of successful people who are shy, then it can't be all bad. Could shyness actually help people succeed? I discovered the answer is yes. Shy people often spend a lot of time alone, putting many hours into reading, learning, focusing, using their imaginations, and getting good at something, all of which help success.

Wayne Schuurman, president of Audio Advisor, told me that being shy helped him become an expert in his field: "I am shy. The whole audiophile community is reclusive. In order to be really good at it, you have to spend a lot of time alone listening to equipment and music."

By hanging out at a party, you may pick up a hot date, but you won't pick up any of the cool skills that require a lot of concentration and practice on your own. **Arthur Benjamin**, "America's Best Math Whiz," told me that being shy helped him hone the skills that made him famous: "I spent a lot of time alone because I was kind of socially awkward. I wanted kids to play with me, but I wasn't the first pick for the football team. So I spent a lot of time doing math and practicing magic tricks. I really enjoyed it. And when I learned magic, I got a lot of attention. I went from just being a nerd to, 'Hey, show us a trick.'"

So shyness isn't all bad, even though it might feel that way at times. In a strange way, shyness can also pay off in a crowd, because shy people spend more time listening and observing than talking. So if you're shy, you may not be the life of the party, but you might see what's going on at the party better than others. One of my heroes, **Albert Maysles**, said to me, "When I was young I was tongue-tied and very shy. It was terribly painful not being part of the group and not having any dates, but it gave me the ability to be more observant, and a listener, and a watcher. I trained myself to see things that other people don't see and I developed a very sharp eye for what should be filmed." And that shy, sharp eye made Albert one of the world's great documentary filmmakers.

But Albert also said, "I am not shy anymore. As a documentary filmmaker, being shy is not what you want because it limits your opportunities." Yes, many opportunities come through interaction with other people, and if we're too shy to open our mouths we miss out on those opportunities. So keep the good things you learn from being shy, but keep pushing yourself through the shyness. Use it then lose it.

I was shy as a child. And when you're shy, you learn to be quiet and absorb what's going on around you, which is important.

Irene Pepperberg expert on parrots' cognitive abilities

I was shy as a kid and I still am. When you're shy and an introvert, you spend more time internally with the ideas in your head and you really focus.

Chris Anderson chairman, TED conference

I was very shy as a kid. I spent my childhood pretty much as a nature nerd, and I spent a lot of time outside by myself. But I developed a sense of focus, an ability to see the patterns in the natural world.

Janine Benyus biologist, educator, author of "Biomimicry"

TO GET OVER SHYNESS
PUSH YOURSELF IN FRONT OF PEOPLE

Shyness has some good things going for it, but if we stay inside our cocoon, it's hard to become a butterfly and really go places. So how do we get over our shyness? It's all about practice, practice, practice. Just keep pushing yourself to talk to others, whether it's one person or a group. And sorry, it's one thing you can't practice alone in your room.

Author and CNN reporter **Meredith Bagby** said to me, "I was the shyest kid around. So to get over it I put myself in situations such as debating, where I was forced to get up in front of an audience and speak." Bell Mobility chairman **Bob Ferchat** used a different strategy: "I was diagnosed as shy, inarticulate, and I also had significant speech impediments. I stammered when I got in front of a group and I'd be so nervous I could barely speak." Gee, you'd think Bob would just lock himself away in a room and never come out. But instead, he did just the opposite: "To get over it I became a teacher and began to give lectures. And, over time, your fear and shyness go away, and speaking even becomes a strength."

People in some professions tend to spend more time in front of computer screens than talking to people. Boston Scientific founder **John Abele** was like that, but he told me he kept pushing himself to get out and interact: "When I got out of college, I was more of a technical guy and I was very shy. So I put myself in situations where I had to deal with people. By pushing myself to do that I gradually became more comfortable. And by the way, it's fun."

Personally, I was shy for most of my life. My relatives tell me I didn't speak to anybody until I was 30. But when I started my company, I thought the shyness could hold me back, so I took a Dale Carnegie course in public speaking. It was great because it pushed me to practice and give a short speech every week. I discovered the more I talked to people, the more the shyness vanished. Soon I felt more comfortable interacting with people and I even gave talks to audiences of thousands of people.

But over time I fell back to my old habits and stopped interacting as much, and the shyness, always lurking, ready to pounce, returned. I learned: If you don't use it you lose it. So I took another Dale Carnegie course, and now I practice talking to people every chance I get. I chat with cabdrivers and people in elevators. I know the names of the staff at my local coffee shop and yak with them a little each day. Every interaction is a chance to practice pushing through the shyness.

So, if you're shy, push yourself to get out there and practice talking to people. Oh, and don't worry about putting your foot in your mouth. By pushing past shyness, your foot will be taking a giant step towards success.

> **I am less shy now than I used to be, because I have been thrust in front of more people than I had ever imagined...like Steven Spielberg and George Lucas. You learn very quickly, if you want that opportunity you can't afford to be shy.**
> *Robert Ward senior VP, Universal Studios*

> **I made presentations to groups of 5 or 10 people for years. Then I pushed myself into circumstances where I have to talk to 300 people. I just said, "What's the worst that can happen?"**
> *Russell Campbell president, ABN AMRO Canada*

PUSH THROUGH

SELF DOUBT

Another internal barrier we need to push through is self-doubt. I discovered that many great people have tremendous self-doubt and insecurity – they just keep pushing through it. **Goldie Hawn** said to me, "I always had self-doubts. I wasn't good enough. I wasn't smart enough. I didn't think I'd make it." But she pushed through the doubts and became an Academy Award-winning actress and film producer.

Drew Nieporent said, "I'm always questioning. I have tremendous self-doubt." Yet he pushes through it and has created some of the world's best restaurants. Then there's **Mike Myers**. Even though he's an Emmy Award-winning comedian and actor, he says, "I still believe that at any time the no-talent police will come and arrest me." Bestselling author **Jane Urqhuart** says, "I don't think any writer, any time in their career, feels secure about their work. We're a very insecure bunch." I could fill these pages with similar quotes, but you get the point. If you have a self-doubt, if you think you're no good, don't worry – you're not alone. Just keep pushing through it and don't let it stop you. Here are 4 strategies successful people use that might help:

1. The "Done It Before" strategy: When you encounter self-doubt, briefly look back at your successes and accomplishments. Don't linger too long in the past, just look at similar things where you succeeded, so you can say, "I've done it before. I can do it again." It works for **Tiger Woods**. He says when he has a high-pressure putt "all I'm thinking about is, 'You've done this a thousand times on the putting green. Just step up and relax and hit the putt.'" **Diane Bean**, senior VP of business development for Manulife, told me, "It's experience. At first you think, 'Oh, I don't know anything and I'm going to screw it up.' And then you learn to figure it out and you go on to the next one. After a while you realize that while you don't know anything about it now, you will know something about it and be able to manage it."

2. The "Outrun It" strategy: Here you forget about the self-doubt chasing you, and keep moving forward so fast that you leave it in a trail of dust. Famous novelist **Stephen King** uses this strategy. He says, "There's plenty of opportunity for self-doubt. If I write rapidly, putting down my story exactly as it comes into my mind...I find that I can keep up with my original enthusiasm and at the same time outrun the self-doubt that's always waiting to settle in."

3. The "Confident/Doubt" strategy: Here you counter-balance the times you really doubt yourself, with the times you're full of confidence. Grammy Award-winning musician **Gary Burton** describes it well: "I think every artist bounces between I'm great and I'm shit. There are moments when you feel like, 'Oh man, I'm lucky I got this far.' Then you switch gears and do something you're really happy with, and you think, 'This is really great!'" Acclaimed graphic novelist **Seth** uses the same approach: "I fluctuate between believing I'm creating a good book and the black dread that each page I'm drawing is slowly revealing what a dim-witted, sentimental idiot I am." The trick with the "Confident/Doubt" strategy is to keep bouncing back and forth between the two. Don't stay on one side too long.

4. The "Sleep It Off" strategy: Amberwood Productions CEO **Sheldon Wiseman** says, "I have self-doubts. Many of them are horrendous and you wonder if you can persevere, but I don't let them overwhelm me and I get over them quite quickly. A good night's sleep helps. When I'm fresh I can do almost anything."

Hey, maybe I'll try the "Sleep It Off" strategy. I need something, because at this moment I really have serious doubts that I'll ever be able to come up with a good ending for this page. So goodnight!

DON'T LOSE ALL YOUR SELF-DOUBT

I'm not good enough!

SELF DOUBT

IT COULD PUSH YOU TO GREAT SUCCESS

It's important to push through your self-doubt so it doesn't stop you from moving forward. But, a word of caution: Don't lose all your self-doubt, because it could actually help push you to great success. I mean, often there's a reason we doubt ourselves. If the voice in my head is saying, "I'm not good enough," maybe it's right. Maybe I'm not good enough and I have to get better. Animation film director **Robin Budd** says, "I find most really talented people are incredibly insecure. They're always thinking that they're not really that great. There's always something gnawing at them inside, but that's also a motivating factor that pushes them forward."

Nicole Kidman has won an Oscar for Best Actress, yet she says, "Every time I star in a film, I think I cannot act. I can always come up with a list of actresses who would do better and try to convince the director to cast someone else." But when Nicole gets the role, that self-doubt pushes her to do great work. Famous architect **Frank Gehry** says, "I approach each project with a new insecurity, almost like the first project I ever did. I get these sweats." Frank actually calls it a "healthy insecurity" and it has helped make him one of the world's great architects. It's as if, instead of security blankets, many successful people have insecurity blankets that keep them from sitting back and resting on their laurels.

Stefan Sagmeister, a famous graphic designer who has created album covers for top bands, including the **Rolling Stones**, said to me, "I have self doubts, and I have enough meetings with rock stars to see that all of them also have serious self-doubts. I thought it was something that would go away with success, but I think it's always there." When Stefan told me that, I had an instant flashback to a few years ago when the Rolling Stones played at a small club before taking their big show on the road. I was a few feet from the stage, and when Mick and the boys walked out you could see the self-doubt on their faces. I couldn't believe it! The world's greatest rock and roll band and they had no idea if the fans would still like them. And it wasn't until they started playing and the crowd went wild that you could see the self-doubt literally melt from their faces and they actually smiled. But I think it's that self-doubt that has kept the Stones working hard and on top for so many years, while more confident bands are long gone.

So keep pushing through your self-doubt, but never lose all of it, no matter how bad it feels. And it can feel pretty bad. **Donald Sutherland** has acted in over 100 films, yet he says, "I throw up on the first day of every movie." Yech! The great paradox is, this thing that feels so bad can also be the catalyst that keeps you on your toes and pushes you to do your best and succeed. Just try to avoid the throwing up part.

> **There has to be self-doubt or you would never grow as a person. Self-doubt is questioning and you should always be questioning yourself and the world around you.**
> *Darlene Lim* post-doctoral fellow at NASA

> **You have to have the self-doubt to allow you to look at the work critically and try to make it better.**
> *Seth* acclaimed graphic novelist

GET A **GOAL** TO PUSH YOU

We've looked at some internal barriers we need to push through on the road to success, like shyness and self-doubt. Now let's look at some strategies successful people use to push themselves. Different strategies work for different people, so use what works for you.

Setting a **GOAL** is one strategy that can push us to get moving. **Norbert Frischkorn**, president of Frischkorn Audiovisual, told me he pushes himself from goal to goal: "I need a goal to push for. Then I reach that plateau, and I go look for another goal." **Jerry Hayes** said he used goals to push his optometry practice to more success: "When I started my practice I didn't see the kind of growth that I thought would happen. But as soon as I started setting very defined goals based on specific accomplishments, by a specific time period, the forward progress was exciting!"

The good thing about goals is they push you to do things you may not like to do, but are necessary to get what you want. Comedian and actor **Rick Mercer** said, "I failed memorization in school. But when I had the goal of getting up on stage, I pushed myself to do memory work, and I could memorize an hour-and-a-half monologue." Having a goal also pushed **Randall Larsen** to do better in school: "I realized I really wanted to fly air force jets, but I couldn't do it without a college degree. So even though I wasn't a very good high school student, I got my college degree in less than 3 years, while I was also working 40 hours a week. It wasn't so much the degree I was after. I had a goal. I had to have that sheepskin to be an air force pilot." Thanks to the pushing, Randall became an accomplished pilot with many military decorations, including the Distinguished Flying Cross and 17 Air Medals.

Eva Vertes was barely a teenager when she gave herself the goal of discovering a cure for Alzheimer's disease. She just kept pushing towards that goal, and it paid off when she discovered a compound that prevents the death of brain cells, a step toward curing Alzheimer's. For her breakthrough, Eva was awarded $30,000 at the Intel International Science and Engineering Fair. Wow! Not bad for a 10th grade science project. Eva says, "I push myself and set impossible expectations. And that pushes me more. It's important to have that level of pushiness. If it's your own goal, then you'd better be the one pushing, because no one else will push you to get to that goal."

So, if you're having trouble pushing yourself, get a goal to push you. Like Eva, it might lead you to discover something – what you're really capable of achieving in life.

> **Goal setting is not a mind game. It is a process of developing the internal willpower to accomplish what you have set out to do.**
> *Joan Samuelson Olympic marathon gold medalist*

> **It's important to have a goal, no matter what that goal is – something out there that you're pushing for, stretching for.**
> *John Girard CEO, Clickability*

> **I have to practice the violin for hours each day. Sometimes it can be difficult to get through an entire session. I just have to keep on remembering what I'm doing it for – the goal.**
> *Adrian Anantawan virtuoso violinist with only one hand*

GET A **CHALLENGE** TO PUSH YOU

A second strategy to push yourself is to set yourself a **CHALLENGE**. What's the difference between a goal and a challenge? The way I see it, challenges are goals with adrenaline added. A challenge has to scare you a little.

Virgin Group CEO **Richard Branson** says, "My interest in life comes from setting myself huge, apparently unachievable challenges and trying to rise above them." Richard rose to the challenge, literally, when he tried to be the first to fly a hot-air balloon across the Atlantic Ocean. (They say a lot of CEOs are full of hot air and Richard took full advantage of it.) He experienced the fear part of the challenge when his balloon hit the jet stream and was being buffeted at 200 mph: "We were crossing every finger, praying that the balloon would hold together." Richard ended up dumping in the North Atlantic and survived to go after other challenges.

Filmmaker **James Cameron** also pushes himself by setting difficult challenges, such as creating special effects that have never been seen before on the big screen. Meeting those titanic challenges took James to the top of the world when his movie *Titanic* won Oscars for Best Picture and Best Director. No wonder he says, "The more the challenge...the more I enjoy it."

Musician **Ed Robertson** of the Barenaked Ladies told me he pushes himself with challenges a little more than his wife would like: "I love wave boarding and snow boarding. I like adventure. Doing that sort of stuff keeps you human and humble." Ed's latest challenge was getting his pilot's license: "It was challenging to do something that was really hard and I wasn't necessarily cut out for. But I felt as much satisfaction from getting my pilot's license as I did from selling 6-million records. I worked at something and achieved it. It made me proud and happy."

Adrenaline doesn't just come from challenges in the air, the wild, or on a movie set. Many people get an adrenaline rush from challenges in the office. Manulife Senior VP **Diane Bean** said, "I like new challenges and I think that pushes me. I like the adrenaline." In retail, Sleep Country founder **Gord Lownds** said, "Sometimes I set impossible tasks and challenge myself to do them." And in the operating room, surgeon **Douglas Dorner** said, "I think surgeons like to be challenged. I've always liked a challenge."

The challenge for **Stephan Van Dam** was just leaving his home in Switzerland and going to America. He not only went to New York, he became an expert on the city and produces brilliant, award-winning maps. He told me, "As a kid of 21, I came to New York and went through the school of hard knocks. It was a real challenge for me, but I think you need to take on these challenges in order to propel yourself forward."

So propel yourself forward with a challenge. It's both scary and fun, but it can take you to new places in more ways than one.

> **It's not about the money. It's still the challenge of going to work and going out on a limb with new technology.**
> **Norbert Frischkorn** *president, Frischkorn Audiovisual*

> **Not all surfers are big-wave surfers. Those who are have a certain passion and a deep desire to challenge themselves by surfing waves of that magnitude.**
> **Ken Bradshaw** *record for biggest wave ever surfed*

GET A **DEADLINE** TO PUSH YOU

DEADLINES are a third strategy people use to push themselves. Physicist **Maurizio Vecchione** says, "I'm deadline-driven. Things don't get done until the deadline is there." Award-winning photojournalist **Kevin Gilbert** told me, "Gotta have deadlines. If I don't have a deadline, I just procrastinate." Comedian **Rick Mercer** agrees: "I've written hundreds of TV shows, but I also have a file in my computer of things that aren't finished because they don't have built-in deadlines. If I had deadlines, I would do them."

Barry Friedman is one half of the juggling Raspyni Brothers, who aren't really brothers, but they are very funny. When I asked Barry how they keep coming up with great new material for their act, he said, "Man, there's nothing like a deadline for a good push. We just sit there and push our brains, and go, 'We've got to do something new.' And something always comes." If the ideas didn't come they'd be standing in front of a huge audience that's not laughing, wishing they were dead. That's why it's called a deadline.

When you think about it, deadlines should really be called alive-lines because they immediately bring you alive and push you into action. Great music composer and producer **Quincy Jones** says composers usually only write 2 or 3 minutes of music a day, but with the fear of a deadline hanging over their heads they can compose up to 10 or 12 minutes. He says, "There's nothing more terrifying than facing a forty-four, or hundred-piece orchestra, with the producers, directors, and editors looking over your shoulder and having no music to play."

When **J.K. Rowling** started writing *Harry Potter*, it wasn't her publisher who imposed deadlines, it was her baby daughter: "I used to put her into the pushchair and walk her around Edinburgh, wait until she nodded off and then hurry to a cafe and write as fast as I could. It's amazing how much you can get done when you know you have very limited time. I've probably never been as productive since, if you judge by words per hour."

A lot of these examples are in the arts, but deadlines are also critical whether you're launching a business, a product, or a rocket. **Dave Lavery**, the NASA whiz who sends robots to Mars, told me launches cost a fortune in terms of money and effort so they really push you to do your best work: "A spacecraft launch is pretty serious deadline pressure. You've got one chance and you can't miss it. So you'll find a way to make it work, no matter what."

Journalist **Walt Mossberg** agrees. He's constantly under deadline pressure to churn out his personal technology column for the *Wall Street Journal* and he told me, "Deadlines are your friend. Some of the best work people do is done right up against a deadline. It's when your wits are really tested." So take Walt's advice and treat deadlines as your friend. I know what you're thinking – with friends like that, who needs enemies!

I find that being pushed by a deadline actually helps my creativity. I don't like the pressure, but the work that comes out of it seems to benefit.
Robin Budd animation film director

Deadlines are absolutely necessary in a creative environment. The deadline forces you to stop tossing ideas around and start implementing.
Susan Ruptash architect

PUSH YOURSELF WITH **DISCIPLINE**

GO FOR **SELF**-DISCIPLINE

AVOID DISCIPLINE BY OTHER PEOPLE
It could involve big, scary guys with whips

DISCIPLINE BY **OTHERS**

A fourth strategy you can use to push yourself is **DISCIPLINE**. Now, I know what you're thinking: "Discipline! Oh, no!" When you hear that word, you know fun is not involved. But discipline really isn't that bad. It's just saying NO at times. Like saying NO to going out with friends when you need to finish the project, or saying NO to the potato chips when you're trying to lose weight, or saying NO to watching TV when you need to prepare for the meeting.

Issy Sharp, founder of Four Seasons Hotels, says, "I think discipline is very important. It gets you to do things that aren't always as comfortable or pleasant as maybe those other things that you might want to do, but you've got to get them done."

When it comes to discipline, there are 2 options. **1. DISCIPLINE BY OTHERS.** This is the least-preferred method since it may involve big, scary guys with whips pushing you to be disciplined. Instead, go for **2. SELF-DISCIPLINE.** This is the self-service option, where you push yourself. **Dawn Lepore**, CIO of Charles

Schwab, says, "I'm very self-disciplined, maybe too much to tell you the truth, but I think that's important in achieving your goals." Sun Microsystems chief scientist **Bill Joy** is also self-disciplined: "My dad said that everyone ends up taking out the garbage. So it's important to do the hard stuff that's no fun, as well as the easy stuff. It ain't a bed of roses! It requires a lot of self-discipline."

Greg Zeschuk used to be a doctor and now he's "Video Game Developer of the Year." How's that for a switch in careers? Medicine and video games may seem worlds apart, but Greg says being disciplined has helped him succeed in both worlds: "Self-discipline is very important. There are barriers, and the challenge in your life is to climb those barriers and get past them, and you can only do that if you are disciplined."

Self-discipline is how award-winning author and performer **Eve Ensler** pushes herself on stage night after night to perform her wonderful plays: "I wasn't disciplined in my youth, but now I'm very disciplined and I think it's a key part of success. You have to just keep showing up and doing the work." Superstar **Celine Dion** has the self-discipline to keep showing up and also the discipline to keep her singing voice in top shape, including saying NO to ice cream. (Gasp! There go my dreams of being a singer.)

The moral of the story is, use self-discipline to push yourself forward towards success. And if your "self" can't muster up the discipline, then go find some big, scary guy with a whip to help.

> **Pop didn't teach me golf.**
> **He taught me discipline.**
> *Arnold Palmer* golf legend

> **Artists are very disciplined. It's not**
> **a case of waiting for inspiration.**
> **You've got to work.**
> *Ken Danby* renowned realistic artist

GET A **MOTHER** TO PUSH YOU

OR **OTHERS** TO PUSH YOU

A fifth strategy to get yourself going, is to get other people to help push you. I mean, it's not always easy to push yourself – that's why they invented MOTHERS. Jazz pianist **Linda Martinez** said to me, "My mother pushed me. I practiced piano 7 hours a day only because my mother told me to." But now that she's an award-winning pianist playing to huge audiences, she's glad her mother pushed her. Great inventor **Thomas Edison** also had a mother behind him: "My mother was the making of me. She was so true, so sure of me, and I felt I had some one to live for, some one I must not disappoint."

Legendary pop music star **Ray Charles** became blind at the age of 6, but his mother pushed him to be self-reliant. Ray said, "Everything I am today is because of her...At home she made me cook meals, dress myself, haul water, even chop wood with an ax...She used to tell me, 'I may not live to see what you do in this life, but there is one thing I know you will never do: You will never hold a tin cup and beg.'"

When I asked **Frank Gehry**, one of the world's great architects, what led to his success, he said, "I pushed myself." Then he thought for a moment and said, "Well, my mother pushed me. And my client Jay Chiat pushed me harder and harder. So find somebody to push you." Yes, it isn't just mothers, and it isn't just when we're starting out that we need a little push. It always helps to have **OTHERS** nudging us along whether it's a boss, colleague, client, coach or mentor, just to name a few.

Nicole Kidman relies on film directors for a little push. She was preparing to act in *Moulin Rouge* when she had second thoughts, called the director and said, "'I think you're going to have to recast it because there's no way my voice is going to be good enough and I can't do the role and you've made a big mistake.' Luckily, he didn't believe me and he pushed me forward." Yes, all the way to a Golden Globe Award for Best Actress. In the sports world, you can always get a coach to push you. When **Jamal Mashburn** was starting out he asked renowned basketball coach Rick Pitino for a push, saying, "I want to be a professional ball player...I know that in order to get there I have to work hard. You'll make me do that." Rick kept pushing Jamal and he became a star on the basketball court.

So if you're having trouble pushing yourself, remember there's somebody out there who can help push you along. The only problem is, who's gonna push you out the door to find them? Sigh... This success stuff is so complicated.

> **My mother said to me, "If you become a soldier, you'll be a general; if you become a monk, you'll end up as the Pope." Instead, I became a painter and wound up as Picasso.**
> *Pablo Picasso 20th century's most famous artist*

> **I really need a network to push me. My husband is boom, boom, boom – he does things. I need people who keep calling me and saying, "Did you do this? Did you do that?" I really need that support system.**
> *Lakshmi Pratury director, American India Foundation*

GET **COMPETITION** TO PUSH YOU

The sixth strategy to push ourselves is **COMPETITION**. Having competitors hot on his heels is what pushed **Roger Bannister** to become the first runner to break the 4-minute mile. He said, "Clearly, if John Landy hadn't been around and Wes Santee, too, I doubt whether I would have been pushing it as hard as I was. But I knew if I didn't do it, Landy or Santee would do it."

Not that I'm in the same league as those champion runners, but I can relate. My fastest running times have not come when I'm alone on the track, but rather when a keen competitor is hot on my heels. Only then do I dig down and push myself harder than I thought possible.

Hey, even **Oprah** is pushed by competition. She said that when she was training to run a marathon, personal trainer Bob Greene figured out how to get her going: "Now, if Bob wants to push me, he'll say, 'See that woman in the pink suit? You can take her.' And I'll kill myself to run past her. I never realized how competitive I am. But I am."

Sure, sports people are competitive, but how about those scientists? It was competition from another scientist that pushed **James Watson** and **Francis Crick** to discover the structure of DNA. James said, "We kept telling the people in London that Linus

Pauling was going to move on to DNA. If DNA is that important, Linus will know it, he'll build a model, and then we'll be scooped. And boy, I was scared." With that competitive fear pushing them, James and Francis finished first in the race to DNA. (Wild cheering from all the scientists watching the race.)

If you're a filmmaker, every time you go to a movie you see your competition projected on the big screen in front of you. When **James Cameron** went to see *Star Wars* it turned out to be a defining moment, because he saw the cool special effects George Lucas was doing and he said to himself, "Oh, wow, I better get off my butt because somebody is doing this stuff…and they're beating me to it." That competition gave James the push he needed and he went on to become an Oscar-winning filmmaker.

Competition is all about keeping you on your toes and doing your best. So instead of hating your competitors, see them as a pushing force that helps you get the most out of yourself. Go find some competitors and thank them for helping you. Then push yourself so far ahead of them you'll leave them in a trail of dust.

Ultimately, what really drives you is the competitive relationship to someone pushing you, and you respond.
Craig McCaw cellular communications pioneer

I love the competition. I love pushing myself to the limit.
Amber Trotter fastest female cross-country runner in U.S. high school history

Your competitor is a gift. He or she gives you the opportunity to do your best.
Jerry Lynch sports psychologist

I was trying to keep up with the boys or beat them at their own games. I still try to beat the boys in business. I'm very competitive.
Ruth Fertel founder, Ruth's Chris Steak House

GET A
TOR-MENTOR
TO PUSH YOU

AND A
MENTOR
TO SUPPORT YOU

Many people say **MENTORS** were important to their success. While mentors provide a support role, this chapter is about PUSH, so for our seventh strategy to push yourself, let's look at another group of people who don't really support you – they push you, and not in a nice way. I call them **TOR-MENTORS** since they give you a kick in the butt rather than a pat on the back.

Tor-mentors are people who bully you, ridicule you, or put you down. You can let them destroy you or you can use them as a powerful force that actually pushes you to one-up them, prove them wrong, or prove yourself. And sometimes that pushes you further than you ever thought you could go.

Great classical violinist **James Ehnes** says he owes his success to a teacher tor-mentor: "My teacher in New York was just a master at pushing the right buttons to get my dander up and force the challenge. And I worked very, very hard because it would have just killed me to think that someone didn't think I was capable of doing something. I'd say, 'Well, I'll show you I'm capable.' And I'd find a way to do it even if it almost killed me."

Bill Bartmann, founder of Commercial Financial Services, had a tormentor in the family: "My sister-in-law was a motivating factor... She didn't want me to date her little sister because I wasn't good enough...and I wanted to prove to this lady that she was wrong...I put her name on a 5-by-7 index card and taped it on the wall directly at eye level. Every night I would raise my head and see her name and that would make me want to put my head back to work."

Basketball superstar **Michael Jordan** was a first-class tor-mentor himself, once called the most psychologically intimidating bully that basketball has ever known. He said he did it to push his teammates to perform better on the basketball court: "If you don't bring your level up to compete with me then I'm going to completely dominate you, and I'm going to talk trash to you and about you while I'm dominating. That's my way of getting my teammates to elevate their game." And Michael's tormenting helped push his team to the top.

My 12th grade math teacher Mrs. Murray was a master tor-mentor. She'd get me up to the blackboard and if I couldn't answer her math question – Whack! – her cane struck me on the back. I really struggled with geometry so I got whacked a lot. But it pushed me to say, "I'll show her!" It made me work a lot harder to understand geometry, and it's interesting that the highest mark on my final 12th grade report card was in Mrs. Murray's math class.

Now, I'm not advocating tormenting anybody. It's no fun. But tor-mentors like Mrs. Murray and my tough clients have pushed me to do some of my best work. So if you find yourself at the mercy of tor-mentors, use them as a force to push you forward. Then when they see how successful you've become it will torment them for the rest of their lives.

> **When I said I was going to go off and do writing a boss said, "You'll be lucky if you ever make a dime." That kind of pushed me to really try and work hard.**
> *Amy Tan bestselling author*

> **Probably one of my biggest motivators was my dad saying I wouldn't amount to anything. I was really pissed off and I think it's been unwinding ever since, just to prove him wrong.**
> *Edward Burtynsky renowned photographer*

PUSH OUT OF YOUR COMFORT ZONE

One of the nice things about success is it brings comfort. Maybe it brings you a more comfortable house, car, furniture, vacation, or life. But here's the paradox – success brings you comfort, but you can't be comfortable and successful at the same time. That's why you see billionaires, who could easily sit back and get comfortable, go to a lot of trouble to keep pushing themselves out of their comfort zones and keep challenging themselves.

Richard Branson, billionaire founder of the Virgin Group, could easily sit back in comfort, but he says, "Once we get comfortable as a company, I like to push the boat out again. My wife keeps saying, 'Why? Why? You're fifty. Take it easy. Let's enjoy it.' ...If I put all my money in the bank and drink myself to death in the Caribbean, I just think that would be a waste of the fantastic position I've found myself in."

Wise move Richard, because many people have risen to the top then slipped into their comfort zones and gone crashing to the bottom. **Linda Evangelista** was one of the world's top supermodels until she fell into her comfort zone and said, "I don't get out of bed for less than $10,000 a day." That was the end of her career. When author **Truman Capote** wrote *In Cold Blood* he became the most famous writer in America. Then he fell into his comfort zone, never finished another book, and died of complications from alcoholism. Boy, that comfort zone is a dangerous place to be!

Award-winning photojournalist **Kevin Gilbert** said to me, "I love the comforts of life, but I don't want to get too comfortable, because then you get lazy and I would rather be on edge a little bit. When I get too comfortable, I need to move on, try new things, be in different places." **Brad Edwards**, director of research at the Institute for Scientific Research, told me a lot of scientists lose their edge when they slip into their comfort zones: "You have to keep pushing. Once you back off, you stop progressing. I've seen lots of good scientists get to a certain point, then just take it easy. And that's basically where they stay for the rest of their careers."

Marketing consultant **Leslie Westbrook** says staying out of your comfort zone is all about growth: "If you are always seeking to be comfortable, you'll have a very limited life. If you're willing to face discomfort, then you'll always grow and you'll always expand your boundaries." Bell Mobility chairman **Bob Ferchat** agrees: "If you go through life feeling comfortable, you won't grow. You create discomfort for yourself because you want to grow in some way." Bob's right. I mean, just ask any baby with new teeth coming in.

So, if you've been sitting with your feet up, feeling cozy for too long, it's time to push yourself out of your comfort zone. If you're uncomfortable speaking to groups of people, then go speak to a group. If you're uncomfortable cycling, then hop on a bike. Whatever you're uncomfortable doing, go do it, and be prepared to grow. So, excuse me while I go take out the garbage. Hey, it's a start!

> **You only ever grow as a human being if you're outside your comfort zone.**
> *Percy Cerutty* renowned running coach

> **The ultimate measure of a man is not where he stands in moments of comfort, but where he stands at times of challenge and controversy.**
> *Martin Luther King Jr.* great civil rights leader

8 TO BE GREAT

1. **PASSION**

2. **WORK**

3. **FOCUS**

4. **PUSH**

5. **IDEAS**

6. **IMPROVE**

7. **SERVE**

8. **PERSIST**

5. IDEAS

Great people come up with IDEAS that light their way to success. One little idea has taken many people from the bottom to the top. We don't have to be "creative" to come up with good ideas. It's all about doing simple things, like keeping our ears and eyes open, being curious, and asking questions. We need to come up with a hundred really bad ideas before – BOING! – we get a great one. So become a fountain of ideas.

IDEAS
LIGHT
THE
WAY
TO
SUCCESS

The fifth trait that makes people great is IDEAS. Ideas are a powerful source of mental energy, and if you can generate better ideas, you have the energy to go further in life. There was a popular song called "You Light Up My Life." It was referring to a person but it could have been talking about ideas, because a good idea really can light up your life. It worked for **Bill Gates**. He said, "I had an idea, founding the first microcomputer software company." And that little idea made Bill a giant in the world of technology and also the world's richest man.

TV stations used to broadcast the news only a few times a day, but **Ted Turner** wanted to see the news at any time and – BOING! – he came up with the idea for CNN, the world's first 24-hour cable news network. That idea lit Ted's way to success and changed the world of broadcasting. No wonder he said, "I intend to conquer the world, but instead of conquering with bombs I intend to conquer with good ideas." General Electric CEO **Jack Welch** knew the power of ideas. He said, "My job is to find great ideas, exaggerate them, and spread them like hell around the business with the speed of light."

Since ideas light the way to success, it's appropriate that the symbol for an idea is usually a light bulb over somebody's head. (Historical note: Before the invention of the light bulb, candles would appear over people's heads when they had an idea, but everybody's hair kept catching on fire, so Edison invented the light bulb.) The light bulb is a perfect metaphor for ideas because they light the way for us to solve problems, take advantage of opportunities, and move forward. Disney CEO **Michael Eisner** said, "The fragile spark of an idea can spread to become a great work of art, or a movie, or a political movement, or an automobile, or a Space Shuttle, or a new communications technology. But these blazing achievements can only happen if the initial idea is cared for, protected, and nurtured until it is ready to spread."

Coming up with a good idea can lead to many rewards, but Beatle **Paul McCartney** says one of the best rewards is the way it makes you feel: "That creative moment when you come up with an idea is the greatest, it's the best…a magic moment." Advertising guru **Jerry Della Femina** feels the same way: "You create something and you can see it and taste it and feel it. It's addictive."

Ideas don't always come easily. Physicist **Leonard Susskind** told me, "Almost all the time you're confused and you're going nowhere. And then, maybe 5 times in your career, you get that sense of open daylight, that 'Aha!' moment, and you see where to go. It's a short-lived thing, and it's also an addictive high, looking for it, pushing for it." The feeling may be short-lived, but those 5 ideas have made Leonard one of the world's great physicists.

Nobel Prize-winning chemist **Linus Pauling** once said: "The best way to have a good idea is to have a lot of ideas." So don't worry about coming up with "good" ideas, just keep coming up with "a lot" of ideas. One of them might turn out to be good, and then, just like the people on these pages, that little idea will also light your way to big success.

> **When people ask me, "How do I start my own business?"**
> **I say to them, "You have to have an idea that everyone**
> **else thinks is crazy, and you go ahead and do it anyway."**
> *Bill Low* CEO, AudioQuest

> **Man's mind stretched by a new idea never goes back**
> **to its original dimensions.**
> *Oliver Wendell Holmes Jr.* renowned jurist

EVERYONE CAN COME UP WITH
GOOD IDEAS

BUSINESS IS AS CREATIVE AS THE ARTS

Warning! I'm now going to use one of the scariest words in the English language. No, it's not taxes. Are you ready? Brace yourself. It's CREATIVITY! Sorry, I had to say it, because generating ideas involves creativity. The problem is many people think they're not creative because they can't draw or paint. But creativity isn't about being artsy, it's about ideas.

I've worked in both the business world and the art world, and I've found that many business people are just as creative as artists, and in many cases they come up with even better ideas. It's just that their canvas is a spreadsheet or business plan. As **Donald Trump** says, "Deals are my art form. Other people paint beautifully on canvas or write wonderful poetry. I like making deals, preferably big deals. That's how I get my kicks."

Ideas lead to success in every field. When a surgeon is operating, the ability to quickly come up with ideas to solve problems can mean life or death. Surgeon **Douglas Dorner** says, "I think the best surgeons are creative. Every surgical procedure has some slightly different twist and the best surgeons are the ones who come up with ideas to deal with the twists that we're given."

The best athletes are very creative, because they're continually coming up with ideas on how to enhance performance. For example, high-jumpers used to dive forward over the bar until **Dick Fosbury** had the breakthrough idea to turn in the air and go backwards, making it easier for his legs to clear the bar. The Fosbury Flop was anything but a flop. Dick's idea won him a gold medal, set a new Olympic record, and became the high-jump technique still used today.

For many years I was part of the design group in a big corporation and, unlike the stodgy engineers we worked with, we saw ourselves as hotshot creative types able to magically come up with brilliant ideas. Then one day I was struggling to figure out where to put a logo on a building and I just couldn't come up with a good idea. One of those uncreative engineers walked over to my desk, pointed down at the drawing, and said, "Why don't you put the logo over there?" It was the perfect solution, and one of those times when you realize everybody can be creative (yes, even engineers). Crossey Engineering president **Wallace Eley** says, "We're always looking for bright ideas to solve problems and do things. It's just that artists are normally seen as creative and engineers frequently are not. It's a matter of pushing a lot of engineers to be creative."

Award-winning science historian **James Burke** says, "Everybody is a kind of fountain of ideas. If you think about the fact that you've got 100-billion neurons in your brain, you've got one hell of a machine in there." So there's nothing stopping you from getting great ideas, no matter who you are or what field you're in. And there's no magic. The next few pages show some of the simple ways that so-called creative people come up with ideas. Do them and you, too, could become a fountain of ideas.

> **The genius creates good ideas because we all create good ideas. That is what our combinational, adaptive minds are for.**
> *Steven Pinker professor of psychology, MIT*

TO GET IDEAS HAVE A

PR BLEM

BIG IDEAS COME FROM EVERYDAY PROBLEMS

Ideas make people great, but how do the greats come up with ideas? Well, one way is to HAVE A PROBLEM, because big ideas come from everyday problems.

Anita Roddick had a problem when her husband went on sabbatical to South America to ride horses, and she had to support herself and – BOING! – she got the idea to start a little business called the Body Shop, which turned into a really big idea. **Richard Branson** had a problem. He was stranded after his flight to Puerto Rico was cancelled. To solve the problem he phoned around, chartered a plane, then sold one-way tickets to the other stranded passengers, filled the flight, and he actually made a profit – BOING! The light went on in his head and he got the idea to start Virgin Airways.

Sky Dayton told me he had a problem: "I was trying to get connected on the Internet, and I spent 80 frustrating hours with my computer, and the service people wouldn't even answer the phone. I had horrible service and a very frustrating experience." BOING! – The light went on in Sky's head: "I said, I can make this easy and people are going to want it. And I came up with the idea for EarthLink." It was an idea that made Sky a technology star and very rich at a young age.

Michael Jordan had a problem. He wanted to wear his North

Carolina shorts because he felt they were lucky. This wouldn't ordinarily be a problem, except Michael played for the Bulls. BOING! – He got the idea to wear baggier and longer shorts than the other players so he could hide his lucky North Carolina shorts under his Bulls uniform. The idea set him apart, started a craze, and soon every player was wearing longer basketball shorts, which opened up whole new opportunities for sportswear.

If you're feeling a little intimidated by the big names above, remember that many big names were little names until they had a problem and came up with a big idea to solve it. Our own daily lives are full of everyday problems just waiting to be solved. **Michael Smithson's** everyday problem was his 9-year-old grandson kept losing stuff. So Michael came up with the idea for a frozen drink container that kids could wear on their wrists, a simple idea that won him a $5,000 prize in a contest.

Bill Gates once said, "I guess you could say that I approach business as a kind of problem-solving challenge...life's a lot more fun if you treat its challenges in creative ways." So when you've got a big or little problem, do what Bill does and try flipping it around and looking at it as a problem-solving challenge. It may be the last thing you feel like doing, but if you can get those ideas flowing, you'll find problem solving is actually fun. And just like Bill's idea of starting a little software company, you might come up with a great idea that will not only solve your problem, it will change your life.

> **I demystified the creative process. I just saw it as an exercise in problem solving. I went at every single job as a problem to be solved.**
> *Matt Groening* creator of "The Simpsons"

> **I get the most fun out of being given a difficult problem, and coming up with ideas to solve that problem. It's very satisfying to do that.**
> *David Jensen* CEO, Brooklands Executives Recruitment

TO GET IDEAS — BE OBSERVANT

LOOK

EYE-Q CAN BE MORE IMPORTANT THAN IQ

If you want to get ideas, simply LOOK AROUND and be observant. In fact EYE-Q is often more important than IQ. Even **Marilyn vos Savant**, who has one of the highest IQs ever recorded, once said, "To acquire knowledge, one must study; but to acquire wisdom, one must observe."

Ron Rice developed his EYE-Q. He was a lifeguard at the beach, and like all good lifeguards he kept an eye on the swimmers, but he also observed something else: "I saw the suntan lotion being sold and it was all old and mundane. And I thought, even with my limited chemistry knowledge I could make something a hundred times better than what was out there. And I created Hawaiian Tropic and I gave it the Hawaiian atmosphere. It was an instant success." That little observation and idea took Ron from the lifeguard stand to the millionaire's club.

Moving from the beach to Wall Street, **Lise Buyer** told me how EYE-Q helped her become a successful investor: "It isn't about what happens in your office, and it isn't about what numbers you can invent on your computer. It's about what's going on outside your door. Are the kids' sneakers Nikes or are they Reeboks? No amount of computer modeling is going to tell you what people are buying. So my advice is, be observant."

Renowned filmmaker **Terry Gilliam** uses EYE-Q to come up with great ideas. He told me, "When you have creative block, look at the world. When I used to run out of ideas I'd go down to the National Gallery in London and just start walking through and – boom, boom – ideas started coming out of the paintings." You might be thinking, "Hey, Terry is in the visual arts so of course he's observant." Well, people in many other fields also know it's important. **Mae Jemison** says EYE-Q helped her become the first black female astronaut: "My mother always told me you have to be observant." Basketball superstar **Charles Oakley's** godfather said Charles "didn't say much, but he was always observing. Charles has a way of taking everything in." And famous New York City mayor **Rudolph Guiliani** was big on EYE-Q: "I made it my policy to see with my own eyes the scene of every crisis so I could evaluate it firsthand."

EYE-Q even caused physicist **Richard Feynman** to win the Nobel Prize. He was in the Cornell University cafeteria one day when he saw a student throw a plate in the air (must have been before they invented Frisbees). In the book *Surely You're Joking Mr. Feynman!* Richard said, "As the plate went up in the air I saw it wobble, and I noticed the red medallion of Cornell on the plate going around. It was pretty obvious to me that the medallion went around faster than the wobbling." So Richard went away and worked out the motion of the mass particles, which led him to a breakthrough in physics. The diagrams he got the Nobel Prize for came from "piddling around with the wobbling plate." Gee, I look at a plate and all I see is food; Richard looks at a plate and wins the Nobel Prize. Now that's what I call observant!

So to get good at coming up with ideas, I'd say forget about IQ and work on your EYE-Q. As famed New York Yankees manager **Yogi Berra** said, "You can observe a lot by watching."

> **The real voyage of discovery consists not in
> seeking new landscapes but in having new eyes.**
> *Marcel Proust* great writer

EARS ARE ANTENNAS FOR IDEAS

It's amazing how many great ideas come simply by LISTENING. Medical geneticist **Josef Penninger** told me his medical breakthroughs often come by keeping his ears open: "That's the most important thing. Listen to people. It starts you thinking, 'This guy gave me a little idea.' Then you talk to somebody else, and you put it all together."

If you want to be a great songwriter, it pays to listen. **Carl Perkins** wrote "Blue Suede Shoes" after listening to somebody at a high school prom tell his date not to step on his blue suede shoes. "I Started a Joke" was a song without a melody, until one night **The Bee Gees** were flying over Germany and they listened to the hum of the jet engines, which sparked the idea for the great tune. **Paul McCartney** and **John Lennon** got the idea for "A Hard Day's Night" by listening to **Ringo**. He would often get his words mixed up and one night after a grueling concert he said, "Boy I'm knackered. It's been a hard day's night!" BOING! – The light went on in Paul and John's heads, and they went away and wrote one of the Beatles' most popular songs.

Billion-dollar ideas have sprung from just listening in everyday situations. For example, **Bernard Silver** was in a grocery store

110

when he overheard the president of the store asking for help in automating his grocery checkout. BOING! – The light went on in Bernard's head, and he went away and developed the barcode.

Botox, another billion-dollar industry, also came from listening. Apparently the average doctor only listens to a patient for 14 seconds before interrupting. But **Dr. Jean Carruthers** is one doctor who did listen to a patient and it paid off big time. The first use of Botox was to treat muscle spasms and Jean had just injected it into a patient's eyelids, when the patient asked her, "Why didn't you inject my brow?" Jean said, "Well I didn't think you were spasming there." The patient replied, "I know I'm not spasming there. It's just that every time you treat me there, I get this beautiful untroubled expression." BOING! – Jean got the idea to use Botox to reduce wrinkles. No wonder Jean says, "You've got to listen to your patients – number one."

Writers get some of their greatest ideas by listening. Famous novelist **Ernest Hemingway** once said, "I like to listen. I have learned a great deal from listening carefully. Most people never listen." When I asked bestselling author **Robert Munsch** how he got his terrific ideas for children's books, he said, "I worked a long time in daycare and my stories came from really experiencing stuff with kids, and listening to them, and knowing what they like." Renowned comedy writer **Bruce Vilanch** says, "I just listen to everybody. Everybody has some kind of knowledge to impart. Listen and somewhere in there is a nugget of an idea."

So, if you want to come up with some really good ideas, it pays to keep your ears open and listen. Think of your ears as antennas for ideas.

> **The key to success is to get out into the store and listen to what the associates have to say...Our best ideas come from clerks and stockboys.**
> *Sam Walton founder, Wal-Mart*

ASKING QUESTIONS LEADS TO IDEAS

A good way to get ideas is to ASK QUESTIONS. The problem is we're often afraid to ask questions because we think we'll look dumb. But if we want to get great ideas, it's a lot dumber not to ask questions. **Richard Saul Wurman**, a very creative designer who has great ideas, says, "Questions drive all of my work." Scientist **Robert H. Dennard** says scientists are always questioning. Robert made the personal computer possible when he invented DRAM (Dynamic Random Access Memory), but he got his big ideas through DRAQ (Dynamic Random Access Questioning). Asking questions is actually one thing humans can do much better than computers. As great artist **Picasso** once said, "Computers are useless. They can only give you answers."

Simple questions often spark ideas for great inventions. In the early days of photography it took forever to get pictures developed. Then one day **George Land** was walking on a beach, he took a picture with his camera, and his daughter asked a simple question: "Why can't I see the picture right now?" BOING! – George got the idea for instant pictures and invented the Polaroid process.

Gary Hamel, founder and chairman of Strategos, tells about a big idea that happened after another question was asked on a beach: "A guy is down in the Caribbean, and he works for Motorola. He's there with his wife, on an island so remote you can't get a cell signal out, and she turns to him and says, 'Honey, you work for communications company. Why can't I make a call?'" – BOING! – "And out of that comes the idea for point-to-point satellite communication all over the world."

Asking questions helped **Martha Stewart** come up with the ideas that built her home-making empire. **Cindy Galbraigh**, head of sales for TV Ontario, told me she ran into Martha at a trade show and was peppered with questions: "Martha was amazing. She asked me, 'What did you buy? Why didn't you buy this? What made you buy that?' She kept questioning me, but in a nice way. She wanted to know, and I was very impressed by that."

Asking questions will lead to ideas in any field. **Elinor MacKinnon**, chief information officer at Blue Shield, said to me, "I'm best at solving complex problems. In truth, I don't actually solve the problems. All I do is ask a lot of questions that other people hadn't thought of asking. Ask lots of questions." TV host **Gayle King** once said, "I think one of my biggest assets is that from the time I was a little kid, I asked a lot of questions. They used to call it being nosy. I prefer to call it inquisitive." And marketing consultant **Leslie Westbrook** says, "I ask a lot of questions. You listen, and that leads you to the next person, the next question, and you learn along the way. The answer, the path, the direction you need in your life, will appear."

In school they give gold stars for answering questions, not asking them. But when **Isador Isaac Rabi** got home from school his mother would always say, "Did you ask any good questions today, Isaac?" And that attitude helped him get the ultimate gold star, the Nobel Prize for physics. Have you asked any good questions today?

> **The idea for the 3-door coupe came from one of our retailer's sons. He was 8-years old and he asked, "Dad, why don't you have an easier way for me to get my stuff into the car?"**
>
> *Cynthia Trudell first woman to run a U.S. auto company*

BORROW AN IDEA

THEN BUILD IT INTO A NEW IDEA

When we run out of something, like milk, we'll borrow some from a neighbor. Well, when you run out of ideas, do the same thing – BORROW someone else's idea, and then BUILD it into a new idea of your own. Well, to be honest, some people don't call it borrowing – they call it copying. Pulitzer Prize-winning cartoonist and author **Art Spiegelman** says, "Most cartoonists learn their craft by copying other cartoonists." In the newspaper industry, writing is actually referred to as "copy." How's that for honesty?

Great people in every field borrow ideas. EarthLink founder **Sky Dayton** said to me, "I have no qualms about taking somebody else's great ideas and using them. My company EarthLink is no great idea. I just put it together better than anybody else." **Laurie Skreslet** summitted Mt. Everest, and he told me even mountain climbers borrow ideas: "I watched other people climb and tried to figure out what allowed them to be efficient. What was it they were doing? And I'd try to emulate that."

I remember when I was young and idealistic, I thought copying was bad. But then I worked in advertising and design, and I discovered only amateurs feel bad about copying; professionals do it all the time. Creative people copy so much that creativity should really be called "copytivity." Some of the greats, like famous artist **Picasso**, actually come right out and admit they steal: "When there's anything to steal, I steal." But no matter what you call it – stealing, copying, mimicking, imitating, or inspiring – I prefer to think of it as borrowing, because eventually you give back when others come along and borrow your ideas.

WARNING Ripping off someone else's idea and calling it your own is called plagiarism (although in Hollywood it's called an honest day's work). So when you borrow be sure to give credit where credit is due.

Starting with somebody else's idea is just another way of charging up the creative battery in your head, sort of like jump-starting your car battery when it runs out of energy. Borrowing gets you going, but then – here's the important part – you need to BUILD what you've borrowed into a new idea. The idea for *West Side Story* was borrowed from *Romeo and Juliet* and then built into a musical format. Aesop borrowed ideas from Indian stories of 2000 years ago and built them into fables. Steve Jobs borrowed the idea for the computer mouse and GUI (Graphical User Interface) from Xerox and created the Apple Macintosh computer. Then Bill Gates borrowed what Steve did and built Windows for PCs. Each of these borrowed an idea and then built it into something great in its own right.

So don't be afraid to borrow an idea and build on it. Who knows, some day somebody might want to borrow your idea. Then you'll know you've really succeeded.

> **We can't afford R&D, so we do R&C, which means Research and Copy.**
> *Pannin Kitiparaporn Dreamworld Theme Park*

> **Don't be afraid to borrow and then modify. There's very little invented from scratch. But be honest about where you got it.**
> *Wayne Schuurman president, Audio Advisor*

TO GET IDEAS
MAKE CONNECTIONS

TAKE ONE THING → ← AND CONNECT IT TO ANOTHER

There's a myth that you get somewhere in life because you know the right people and have connections. But in reality many people achieve success, not by having connections, but by making mental CONNECTIONS between different things. They see or hear one thing and connect it to something else they already know, or a problem they're trying to solve, and – BOING! – they get a new idea. As novelist **William Plomer** said, "Creativity is the power to connect the seemingly unconnected."

Douglas Adams was traveling through Europe with a book called *The Hitchhiker's Guide to Europe*. Then one night as he looked up at the sky, his mind made a connection between the guidebook and the galaxies above him, and BOING! – he got the idea for *The Hitchhiker's Guide to the Galaxy*. It turned into a radio play, bestselling book, popular TV series, and film. So by looking at the stars and making a connection, Douglas became a star himself.

3M scientist **Art Fry** also made a connection that changed his life. Art had a problem because the scraps of paper he used as bookmarks kept falling out of his hymnbook, so in church poor Art was probably always singing the wrong hymn. Then one day

116

he remembered a talk he'd heard about a new adhesive considered a failure because it didn't stick permanently. Art connected his bookmark problem with the low-stick adhesive and – BOING! – he got the idea for Post-it Notes, those sticky pieces of paper that don't stick permanently. They solved Art's problem, became a major product for 3M, and they're something I can't live without.

The Beatles record producer **George Martin** says **John Lennon** was a master at connecting unrelated things and turning them into songs. Once John took a newspaper headline he liked – "4,000 holes in Blackburn, Lancashire" – and started a song. Then he asked **Paul McCartney**, "Do you have anything we can put in the middle of this song?" Paul said he had another song, but it had nothing to do with what John was doing. John said, "It doesn't matter, we can stick 'em together," and – BOING! – "A Day in the Life" was born, one of my favorite Beatles songs.

Advertising guru **Jerry Della Femina** says, "Creativity is about making a lot of quick connections about the things you know, the things you've seen. The more you've seen, the more you've done, the easier it is to make that jump." Bestselling author **Stephen King** says it's a great feeling when you make those connections: "If there's any one thing I love about writing more than the rest, it's that sudden flash of insight when you see how everything connects." And when you connect one and one, they don't just make 2 – they make something new. As Stephen says, "Two previously unrelated ideas come together and make something new under the sun." So, keep looking for those connections, and it will help you connect with success.

> **Make connections. Ask, "How can this relate to that? Maybe if I join these 2 strange things together I'll get something completely new." That's human creativity.**
>
> *Lindsay Sharp director, National Museum of Science and Industry, London*

MISTAKES AND FAILURES
LEAD TO GREAT IDEAS

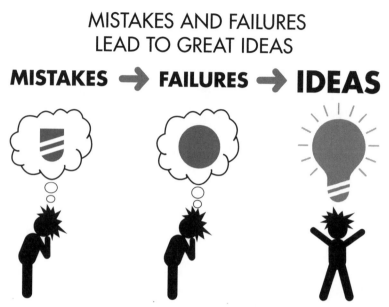

MISTAKES ➡ FAILURES ➡ IDEAS

We're often taught that mistakes and failures are bad. But when it comes to ideas, mistakes and failures are actually good, because it's hard to come up with a great idea without first coming up with many other ideas that really suck. Mistakes and failures are really the seeds for creativity, and that's why Disney CEO **Michael Eisner** said, "You can't succeed unless you've got failure, especially creatively...we encourage movies that bomb, television shows that bomb, Broadway plays that bomb, books that bomb...because only out of that will you be able to have the really big successes."

In the advertising world, author and speaker **Steven Schwartz** quickly learned that mistakes and failures are a necessary part of coming up with ideas: "I still remember my first day on the job in advertising. The art director walked me over to the wastepaper basket and pointed to it and said, 'Don't ever be afraid to use it.'" In the film world, **Robert Altman**, who won an Oscar for his movie *M*A*S*H*, says M*I*S*T*A*K*E*S often bring the best ideas: "I'm looking for mistakes. Shelley Duvall's skirt got caught when she slammed a car door in *Three Women*. I said, 'Great! Leave it in!'" Yes, I remember seeing the film and I thought that mistake was the most memorable moment.

A fear of making mistakes is a big mental barrier to coming up with ideas. Renowned illustrator **Philip Burke** told me that being afraid to flub held him back at first, but he managed to get over it: "I now think it's okay to make mistakes, so I may start something, get halfway through, and just erase it all and start again. I learned if it's not working wipe it out now. If it's still not working, wipe it out again. I might wipe out my entire cartoon 10 times." All that wiping out meant Philip's career didn't wipe out, and he was commissioned to do amazing portraits of Madonna and other stars for magazines like *Rolling Stone* and *Vanity Fair*.

The typical symbol for ideas is a light bulb over somebody's head. But a trash can would also be a great symbol, because a whole bunch of ideas get trashed before we can get to that "Wow" idea. When immortal scientist **Albert Einstein** went to teach at Princeton, they asked him what he wanted for his office and he replied, "A desk, some pads and a pencil, and a large wastebasket to hold all of my mistakes." Einstein realized the importance of mistakes and wasn't afraid to make them. In fact, his most famous formula, $E = mc^2$ didn't start out that way. In his manuscripts you can see where he first wrote $N = 1/c^2$. He eventually realized his mistake and scribbled in $E = mc^2$. The rest, as they say, is history.

So, if you want an idea that goes down in history, churn out a lot of ideas that get trashed. You've gotta produce a lot of garbage before you end up with gold.

If you fail early and often, and persevere through it, that's often where you can make creative breakthroughs.
Steve Jurvetson renowned venture capitalist

A word processor is one of the greatest inventions of all time. The minute the word processor came out I could make the world's biggest mistakes, then fix them later.
Terry Gilliam great filmmaker

WRITE DOWN IDEAS

BEFORE THEY FLY AWAY

I'm now going to let you in on one of the biggest secrets to ideas. Are you ready? Okay, here it is: When you get an idea, write it down. That's it? Yes, that's it. The world's greatest idea isn't much good if you can't remember what it was. Four Seasons Hotels founder **Issy Sharp** said to me, "If an idea comes up I will always, always, stop and make a note, wherever I am, even at dinner."

Top real estate agent **Elli Davis** said, "Even though I have a good memory, I still write everything down. 'The faintest ink is better than the best memory.'" Comedian **Sinbad** can memorize an hour-long comedy routine, but when he gets an idea it will vanish in a flash unless he captures it: "I've had ideas and I'll call my secretary to tell her, and then go, 'Damn, I forgot the idea.' So now when I say something, I write it down. I'll be at dinner with somebody, and I'll just grab a napkin and start writing." Respected travel writer **Pico Iyer** says, "A discipline I have is that I take down a huge amount of notes then and there. I don't wait, even until the next day, because by the next day it's often forgotten."

Bob Dylan didn't pull his great ideas for songs out of the air – he pulled them out of a box! **David Hajdu**, author of *Positively 4th Street,* says, "Dylan has his antennae up all the time...he writes down phrases people say to him, or things he overhears in restaurants, then puts them in a box. Whenever he needs a song, he reaches into the box and pulls something out." Instead of a box, Bell Mobility chairman **Bob Ferchat** pulls ideas out of his briefcase: "I'll write ideas down on a slip of paper and throw them in my briefcase. They accumulate, then I add them to my research pile."

Oh, and don't worry about what you write on. I even scribble ideas on toilet paper (which some people say appropriately reflects the quality of my ideas). Guitarist **Jimi Hendrix** jotted down ideas on everything from napkins to the backs of envelopes. Author **Stephen King** was asleep on a plane when he had a dream. He says, "I wrote it on an American Airlines cocktail napkin so I wouldn't forget it, then put it in my pocket," and that idea turned into his bestselling novel *Misery*. Even successful high-tech people use low-tech napkins. **Elinor MacKinnon**, the CIO in charge of all the computer technology at Blue Shield, says, "When I meet and talk with people I always scribble on napkins, then file them at work."

I've learned from all these great people, so now I always carry a little notebook and a couple of pens, in case one runs out of ink. And I also carry a small digital recorder. I'll tell you, if I ever get a great idea, there's no way it's gettin' away from me. The bottom line: If you want to move up to success, write down your ideas.

> **One secret to success I found the hard way is incredibly basic. Write everything down, leave nothing to memory. Memory gets you in trouble. Memory ultimately betrays you.**
> *Rick Pitino renowned* basketball coach

> **Don't you wish you could make your brain bigger? You can. Buy a notebook. I write things down. Writing is part of your digestive process for ideas. When you put it in your notebook you digest it to the next level.**
> *Bob Rogers founder, BRC Imagination Arts*

HOW I GOT
A BIG IDEA

There's no magic to coming up with ideas. Just do the simple things shown on these pages. How do I know? Because that's how I came up with a really big idea that won top international video awards. It started when my company was asked by a leading telecommunications corporation to produce a series of speeches and videos to be shown at a huge conference on the future of the telephone network. A lot was at stake for our clients, so our work had to be great. But my colleague Thom and I had a problem. How could we make ugly telephone switches and boring network diagrams interesting and understandable? We needed a great idea to bring the messages to life.

We kept our eyes open and **LOOKED** around, at big things like the trends in the industry, and little things like what our clients had on the walls of their offices. We **LISTENED** for weeks while dozens of technology experts told us about the future of communications networks. We **ASKED QUESTIONS**, lots of dumb questions. We read hundreds of research reports, magazines, books and newspaper articles. We kept coming up with ideas and, even if they weren't good, we **WROTE DOWN EVERY IDEA.** The deadline loomed, the pressure to produce increased, but we still didn't have that big eureka idea. We still needed a "Wow!"

Then one day we were on a flight to Atlanta, dead tired from working 20-hour days. I was staring out the window at the sky and Thom was telling me how optical fiber converted voice and data into electrons that could be sent through the phone network at high speed, and –BOING!– suddenly my mind made a **CONNECTION** between electrons and airplanes and it sparked an idea. I pictured us in a jumbo jet, but we were flying through fiber optics, and we weren't people, we were electrons that made up a phone call. I realized the whole story could be told from the perspective of electrons traveling inside the telephone network. We had our breakthrough idea! And we knew we could make it interesting, funny, and easy for the audience to understand.

I wrote the scripts, we dressed up actors as electrons, and then filmed them in jumbo jets and airports. While we were doing this I realized that 10 years earlier I'd seen a movie where people were dressed as sperm and were traveling on a plane. So maybe my subconscious mind **BORROWED** an idea from an earlier time and **BUILT** it into something new. All I know is the metaphor worked marvelously. The video was a huge hit with audiences and won awards around the world for best corporate video and script.

I want to emphasize that I'm no creative genius. I'm just an ordinary guy. When I first started my career I couldn't come up with a good idea if my life depended on it. But then I started working with people who were creative. I watched them and started copying the things they did, like problem solving, listening, observing, trying to connect different things together, and writing ideas down. And slowly over time my ideas got better and better.

So take it from me, anybody can be creative. Just do the same things that all the successful people on these pages do, and a big idea will come to you too.

8
TO BE
GREAT

1. **PASSION**

2. **WORK**

3. **FOCUS**

4. **PUSH**

5. **IDEAS**

6. **IMPROVE**

7. **SERVE**

8. **PERSIST**

6. IMPROVE

Great people are on a never-ending mission to IMPROVE themselves and what they do. Improvement means getting really good at something, and then making it better and better. The big key to improvement in anything can be summed up in 3 words – practice, practice, practice. Always aim to do the best you can, and that can take you to being the best there is.

KEEP **IMPROVING**

The sixth trait that makes people great is IMPROVE. Successful people are on a never-ending mission to improve, whether it's their project, their product, their service or themselves. Improvement is so important that the corporate world even came up with a buzzword for it – Continuous Improvement. As FedEx founder **Fred Smith** once said, "Our management system is built on continuous quality improvement...we've got to get better and better year after year."

Continuous Improvement helped **Amy Tan** become a bestselling author. She told me, "I have a willingness to improve and always learn." Continuous Improvement helped **Sandra Ainsley** build a successful art gallery: "In my mind, every day I'm trying to figure out how I can improve. I think that's important. You always have to strive to be better and to be more creative." Continuous Improvement helped quadriplegic **Sam Sullivan** become mayor of Vancouver: "People complain that I'm always changing things. Why can't I just leave them alone? But I can't do that. If I see it's not working perfectly, I want to adjust it a bit, rethink it a bit. Improve it." Reminds me of a book title by great industrial designer **Raymond Loewy**, *Never Leave Well Enough Alone.*

The world of sports is all about Continuous Improvement. Golf superstar **Tiger Woods** said, "You know, December 31, if I can say that I'm a better player now than I was January 1 of the same year, then it was a successful year, because in the end if you keep doing that, each and every year, you are going to have one heck of a career." Basketball superstar **Michael Jordan** was an improvement machine. Chicago Bulls assistant coach John Bach said, "Michael had that rare capacity to be a genius who constantly wanted to upgrade his genius."

Improvement is as important in the classroom as it is on the basketball court, and not just for students. Professor **Brian Little** says, "You are always looking for what might be improved. Is there anybody bored over here? Have I missed doing this particular aspect of the presentation? Could I sort of tweak it a little bit next lecture?" Gee, I wish my teachers had taken whatever he's taking. No wonder students at Harvard voted him "Most Popular Professor."

Science and technology is driven by Continuous Improvement. **Robert H. Dennard**, the scientist who invented Random Access Memory and made the personal computer possible, says scientists have a fundamental belief that anything can be improved. Yes, thanks to guys like him, the minute I buy a computer, the next day there'll be a new improved one that does twice as much for half the cost. And that's a good thing, or I'd still be writing on a clay tablet.

So even though it's a corporate buzzword, I like the concept of Continuous Improvement, because successful people keep improving themselves, their skills, and their work – and it never stops. Pioneer fabric designer **Jack Lenor Larson** was in his 80s when I asked him what he wanted to do for the rest of his life. He simply answered: "I want to keep on improving."

> **I never pick up an item without thinking of how I might improve it.**
> *Thomas Edison* inventor of the light bulb

> **At the end of the day you'd like to say, "Gee, I improved in this way today."**
> *Sherwin Nuland* professor of surgery, Yale

GET REALLY REALLY GOOD AT WHAT YOU DO

Continuous Improvement means doing three things: 1. Getting **GOOD** at what we do. 2. Keep getting **BETTER**. 3. Aiming to do our **BEST**.

But don't great people aim to do "Great?" Some do. Architect **Susan Ruptash** says, "You always push for great in every aspect of what you do. You can't hit great every time, but you don't give up trying to do great next time." But it's interesting that in my research not many great people actually use the word "great." They focus on good, better, and doing their best, and that leads them to greatness. So let's start with GOOD.

Alex Garden, CEO of Relic Entertainment, sums up "Good" when he says, "The best chance you have to be successful is to put your nose down in something and get damn good at it." Alex has won over 50 awards including the prestigious "Game of the Year" award, so putting his nose down and becoming a good game developer helped him succeed.

There's a lot of satisfaction we get from being good at what we do, and that helps fuel success. CNN reporter and author **Meredith Bagby** says, "There is something satisfying about being the good writer, the good speaker, the good mathematician. It's the self-satisfaction that you get after completing a project that you are proud of." Animation film director **Robin Budd** knows that feeling. He says, "I definitely want to excel. Not for the sake of being better than someone else, but just because it's so satisfying to do something well. It's really tough to make it shine, but there is no other feeling like it. All the struggle is worth it for that moment of Wow!"

Singer/songwriter **Bruce Cockburn** says, "Step one is to be as good as you can be, at whatever you pick to do. Obviously, if you are not good at it, nobody is going to be interested." When you do good work, people do show an interest in you, and you earn their respect, no matter what the job. Renowned filmmaker **Norman Jewison** told me about a man who sweeps the streets in his area: "Everybody respects him simply because he does a good job. He cares about what he does and he takes pride in the fact that his area of the street is cleaner than anybody else's."

Unfortunately, not everybody wants to do a good job, but that just leaves more opportunity for those who do. **Paul Bunt** runs a successful traffic engineering company and he says, "If you do something well, you'll be rewarded. That alone will be enough to distinguish you, because there are so many people who don't seem to care."

Successful people do care, and often they care more about doing a good job than about fame or success. **Marvin Hamlisch** has won 3 Academy Awards for composing such great songs as "The Way We Were," but if you go to his apartment you won't see the Oscars sitting there, because his priority isn't winning gold statues – it's doing good work.

So, don't focus on things like success, money, respect, or awards. Focus on doing really good work and all the other good things will come along automatically.

> **Be as good as you can be at what it is you are.**
> *Murray McLaughlin singer, songwriter*

> **Nobody's a natural. You work hard to get good, and then work hard to get better.**
> *Paul Coffey hockey player, record goals by a defenceman*

MAKE IT BETTER BETTER BETTER

The second aspect to Continuous Improvement is to keep getting BETTER. Three-time Olympian runner **Suzy Favor Hamilton** says, "I can't explain where it comes from, but I have this drive to keep doing better and better." Physicist **Maurizio Vecchione** told me to "Keep setting the threshold higher. So once you've done something, redo it. Don't sit back and say you've done it. Think about how you would do it better."

In the business world, General Electric CEO **Jack Welch** talked about: "A relentless, endless, company-wide search for a better way to do everything we do." That attitude made GE a very successful huge company, and it also works for small companies. **Richard Saul Wurman**, creator of the Access travel guides, told me: "Every time I did a guide book I tried to make it better. I mean, why do it if you can't do it better?"

Beatle **Paul McCartney** is one of the great songwriters, yet he says, "Well, you know, I'm still looking to write a great song...You never think, well, that's enough, or that's good enough." The Rolling Stones' **Keith Richards** says, "I guess we're obsessed with showing that we can still make a better record than we've ever made, and go out and perform it as well as we ever did. Whether or not we really do doesn't matter. It's just going for it and thinking the possibility is there." Successful up-and-coming singer/songwriter **Hawksley**

Workman has the same attitude: "I'm always challenging myself to be better, to strive for some greatness. Why would you want to do anything else, no matter what you do?" In the film world, **Robin Budd** directs wonderful animated films for folks like Disney, and he said to me, "I always try to do it better than I've ever done before, to push it just a little bit farther. Sometimes you'll see a scene up on the screen you thought would work really well, but you know it could be better so you keep honing it and reworking it."

The continuous search to keep getting better and better can mean being dissatisfied a lot of the time. **Oprah** says, "I'm never satisfied where I am in my life. I'm always trying to push the envelope. What is the next level? How I do grow myself to be a better person?" Onex CEO and billionaire **Gerry Schwartz** feels the same way: "We look at ourselves and ask ourselves every day how we can do better. Nobody here feels good about where we are." NOTE: Being dissatisfied doesn't mean being unhappy. Hall of Fame TV producer **Norman Lear** said to me, "I do strive to do better. But I'm not one of those people who's always unhappy if it isn't perfect."

It's just that successful people have this voice in the back of their heads that keeps saying, "Come on. Make it better." And that's a good thing, because success is like a staircase with many levels and it's by getting better that we move from one level to the next. Oh, and sorry, there are no escalators.

You can always take what you have and make it better.
Ted Williams *one of baseball's greatest hitters*

I can't be satisfied with the way I am, the status quo.
You have to keep improving, doing something better.
David Gallo *marine scientist, director, Woods Hole Oceanographic Institute*

It's a lot of work to try to get better, but you just can't quit.
Brian McLeod *blind golf champion*

AIM TO DO YOUR
BEST

Even if you don't always make it!

The third aspect to Continuous Improvement is to always aim to do your BEST. Six-time space shuttle astronaut **Story Musgrave** told me, "You strive to do your best, to be the best you can be all the time." Four Seasons Hotels founder **Issy Sharp** feels the same way: "You're constantly in search of excellence and that never stops. It's just trying to be your best." And surgeon **Douglas Dorner** said it's important to "Be the best you can. If you're going to be a surgeon entrusted with people's lives, you better work as hard as you possibly can and get it right."

Nez Hallett III, CEO of Smart Wireless, told me that doing your best saves regrets: "Whatever I do, I do it to the best of my ability. I don't like regrets, going back later and saying, 'Hey, I didn't give it my best shot.'" Instead of focusing on getting to the top, **Ian Craig** says he focused on doing his best: "Every time I got a job, no matter what it was, I just did the best I could in that job. I never went into a job thinking, 'Gee, if I do great they're going to make me a supervisor.' You just do the best that you possibly can with the job at hand." And with that attitude, Ian rose to the top as president of Nortel Networks wireless division.

Some people not only aim to do their best, they also want to be the best. Champion cyclist **Lance Armstrong** once said, "I want to be the best rider there is...I don't want to just be good at it, I want to be the best." And he succeeded in becoming the best cyclist in the world, 7 times no less. Like Lance, you can aim really high if it works for you. But often we have no control over the factors that lead to being number one and thinking about it can be a distraction. That's why many successful people simply aim to "do their best."

Greg Zeschuk is a good example. He told me, "Instead of saying, 'I'm going to work to the goal of being the best video game developer in the world,' you say, 'I'm just going to try and do my best.' Ultimately, we're just trying to do our best all the time." And by doing his best Greg became the world's best when *Billboard* named him "Game Developer of the Year." Curling champ **Colleen Jones** didn't aim to be the best. She said, "I just want to play as well as I can on that day and leave it with no regrets." With that strategy, Colleen won 2 World Curling Championships and became the best in the world.

One last example is actor **Russell Crowe**. He said to me, "You just want to do the best work you can do." And by always doing his best, Russell became the best, winning an Academy Award for Best Actor. So, don't worry about being the best, or shooting for the stars. Just aim to do the best you can, and that can take you to being the best there is.

> **I wouldn't say I had a specific goal other than to just do the best I could do and I would succeed.**
> *David Cohen* renowned writer for "The Simpsons"

> **Get out there and, whatever you are doing, do it to the best of your ability. No one can do more than that.**
> *John Wooden* legendary basketball coach

PRACTICE PRACTICE PRACTICE PRACTICE PRACTICE PRACTICE

A big key to improvement and getting better can be summed up in 3 words: practice, practice, practice. I mean, when **Lance Armstrong** was asked how he won the world's ultimate cycling race, the Tour de France, for the seventh time, he simply said, "The difference is that my team practices 12 months of the year, not 3 or 4."

The thing to remember is that none of the greats start off being great at something. Practice is the big thing that takes them there. **Laurie Skreslet** made it to the top of Mt. Everest, the world's highest mountain, but he says, "I wasn't good at climbing when I started. It took a lot of practice." Surgeon **Douglas Dorner** told me, "You need years and years of training and practice, so you know how to respond in a difficult situation. Training and practice are the big things, whatever we do."

Renowned pop artist **Peter Max** said, "You've got to practice. You've go to paint very, very hard every day. And after a while it starts to look like something." Astrophysicist **Jaymie Matthews** says even the study of the stars and galaxies takes practice: "You've gotta keep practicing and you've gotta keep pushing yourself to practice."

Personally, I'm always trying to improve my writing. (Hey! Who's that saying, "It's about time?") So whenever I interview writers

I always ask for advice. Award-winning playwright **Eve Ensler** told me it's all about practice: "If you want to be a writer, you have to write all the time. I write every day. I write everywhere I can. It's improving your instrument, it's teaching yourself how to do something better so words come easily, so you know how to put things together, so you can craft things in new ways. It just means practice, practice, practice. Everything's about practice." It also worked for **The Beatles**. They constantly practiced writing. **Paul McCartney** said, "We always wrote a song a day, whatever happened we always wrote a song a day...I think why we eventually got so strong was we wrote so much through our formative period."

It's easier to push yourself to practice if you actually enjoy the process. Classical guitarist **Liona Boyd** says, "I've always loved practicing so it's not a real chore." And no matter how good Liona gets, she says it still takes constant practice: "They say if you don't practice, the first day your hands know it, the second day you know it, and the third day your audience knows it."

Practice is so important that some professions actually call their business a "practice." My lawyer has a "practice." So do my doctor, dentist, and accountant. But since constant practice is the key to getting good at anything, maybe we should all call what we do our "practice."

> **When people ask me about writing, I always say just write, write, write every day. Don't think about becoming a success, or finding a publisher. Just do the practice.**
> *Pico Iyer respected travel writer*

> **We learn by practice. Whether it means to learn to dance by practicing dancing or to learn to live by practicing living, the principles are the same.**
> *Martha Graham great dance choreographer*

Repetition to Excess Produces Success

Improvement is all about practice, and practice is all about REPETITION – doing the same thing over and over again. When I go to the track for running workouts, the coach has us do repetitions or REPS, which means we run flat out for one lap of the track, then die – I mean rest – for 3 minutes, and then repeat the sequence 10 times. It's a killer workout, but reps definitely make you faster.

Basketball players do reps, except they call it shooting hoops. Great basketball coach **John Wooden** made reps the foundation of his training: "I created eight laws of learning: explanation, demonstration, imitation, repetition, repetition, repetition, repetition, and repetition." Cycling champion **Lance Armstrong** trained for the Tour de France by doing grueling reps up steep hills: "There were something like 50 good, arduous climbs around Nice, solid inclines of ten miles or more. The trick was not to climb every once in a while, but to climb repeatedly."

Reps are associated with sports, but they're really the key to improvement in any area. Famous chef **Julia Child** said she did her strawberry souffle "at least twenty-eight times before I finally conquered it." By doing a lot of reps while training for space flights, **Story Musgrave** became the first astronaut to fly on 6 Space Shuttles and cover 25 million miles in space: "I did more practice than I should have. People would haul me away from machines, saying, 'You're gonna wear it out!' I'd repeat exercises

136

so many times the machines exceeded their limits and broke." **Eve Ensler** broke things too, except they were attendance records for her play, *The Vagina Monologues*. Eve says, "It's doing things over and over again. I did the monologues for 5 years, night after night after night, breaking through levels in myself, until I finally got to a place where I wanted to be."

Celebrated children's author **Robert Munsch** has sold over 40-million books and he told me he owes a lot of that success to reps: "Before I do a book, I'll tell stories for years, again and again and again and again. That's how they get good. That's the only way I know how to make stories good." Acclaimed book designer **Chip Kidd** says it's not always fun repeating the same thing over and over, but it's worth it: "The most tiring, and yet the most rewarding experiences, are when you keep redoing it again and again; but what you end up with is actually the best thing."

Business people do reps. I mean, repeat a gazillion emails, meetings, and phone calls, and you find yourself eventually getting good at them. Repetition is so important that sales people are actually called "sales reps." Okay, I admit it really stands for "representatives," but it should stand for "repetition" because that's the key to successful selling.

As you can see from these examples, reps are how people improve and get good, no matter what field they're in. So I'd say REPS really stands for: Repetition to Excess Produces Success!

> **Repetition of action makes greatness. You've got to repeat what you do a lot. Repetition, every day.**
> *Peter Max renowned pop artist*

> **To memorize plays I would read them out loud 5 times a day, every day and repeat and repeat. Even if I'd done a show 100 times, when I had a day off, I would still sit down alone in a room and repeat the whole show out loud.**
> *Rick Mercer award-winning comedian and satirist*

FOCUS ON YOUR STRENGTHS

FORGET ABOUT YOUR WEAKNESSES

Another way to improve and become great is to focus on your strengths. Not everybody knows this little key to success. In a recent survey, over half the respondents said it was more important to work on their weaknesses than their strengths. When I read that I thought, "Gee, that's interesting," because when I ask successful people the same question, they consistently say to go with your strengths and forget about your weaknesses. BCE president **Jean Monty** told me, "Focus on the things you do well. If you're good at computers and not football, don't try to be a football player. And don't be afraid to say you're weak in some areas, so you don't go down a rat hole trying to do something you know you won't be able to do very well."

Respected travel writer **Pico Iyer** said, "Don't psyche yourself out by thinking of all the things you can't do. I mean, I'm a professional writer and I can't type. Don't look at what you don't have, just find what you do have and go with it." **Don Norman**, author of *The Way Things Work*, says it works this way: "Everybody is bad at a lot of things, but everybody has some unique thing they can be the worlds best at. And the trick is to find that unique thing."

Of course, focusing on your strengths will mean you're really bad at a lot of other things. But who cares?

J.K. Rowling has a strength writing great *Harry Potter* novels. Who cares if she was terrible at metalwork in school? J.K. said, "I was the worst in my class – just terrible...I did try, but I just could not do it."

Lance Armstrong has a strength in cycling and it made him a world champion. Who cares if he couldn't play ball? Lance says, "When it came to anything that involved moving from side to side, or hand-eye coordination – when it came to anything involving a ball, in fact – I was no good."

Quincy Jones has a strength composing great music and that has won him countless Grammy Awards. So who cares if he can't drive a car or a nail? Quincy says, "I couldn't drive a nail if my life depended on it." Quincy knows many great people and he says, "In my view the people who achieve greatness in their chosen fields have a core skill upon which they expand."

Let's conclude with **Erik Weihenmayer** who focused on his strength in climbing, ignored his weakness of being totally blind, and climbed to the top of the world's highest mountain, Everest. Erik says, "I made a promise to myself. The things I could not do, I would let go; but the things I could do, I would learn to do well."

The bottom line is you can be really bad at many things, as long as you're really good at one thing. So go with your strengths. Like Erik, that's how you'll climb to success.

> **There's no use trying to fix all our little weaknesses and idiosyncrasies. It's much better to say, "This is what I'm good at."**
> *Josef Penninger acclaimed medical geneticist*

> **In life, I gradually learned the things I was not good at, so I don't put myself in situations where I have to call on them. Instead, I go with the things that I do well.**
> *Gary Burton Grammy Award-winning vibraphonist*

OUTSOURCE YOUR WEAKNESSES

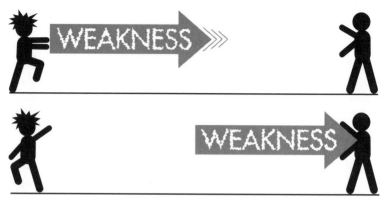

It's important to focus on your strengths and forget about your weaknesses. But the one time you can't forget a weakness is when it will be a big roadblock to your success in a particular area. No matter what field you're in there are usually basic minimum standards that need to be met. I mean, if you're dying to be a surgeon, and you faint at the sight of blood, it will be your patients who end up dying. So how do we handle success-blocking weaknesses? Successful people seem to have 2 strategies:

1. Work on the weakness and fix it. BCE president **Jean Monty** told me he had a weakness in public speaking: "I used to hate standing up and speaking in front of people, but if you want to lead a company you've got to be able to speak in public. So I had no choice. It was a weakness and I worked my ass off on it." I've seen Jean give great speeches to thousands of people, so he fixed his weakness and actually transformed it into a strength.

2. Outsource your weaknesses. The second strategy is to borrow a trick from the corporate world. For example, a company that's strong in product development, but weak in manufacturing, will often outsource their manufacturing and get another company to do it for them. Successful people do the same thing. Umbra cofounder **Paul Rowan** told me his strength was in the creative areas, but he had a weakness in business, so he outsourced it: "I was artistic and I realized really quickly that I needed partners who were better organized and more business-minded, so I had business partners right from the beginning." **Lakshmi Pratury**, director of the American India Foundation, told me she outsourced her weakness in business operations: "Give me an operational person to match me and I'll move mountains. I'm good at the big plan, but to actually make it work, I really need an operations person. It took me awhile to figure that out." Audio Quest CEO **Bill Low** outsourced his weakness in management: "I'm not a manager, so I hired a president to be more professional about creating a structure for the business."

If you can find a person with strengths and weaknesses that are the opposite of yours, you compensate for each other. I have a long list of great duos who made up for each other's weaknesses, including **Lennon** and **McCartney**, **Bill Gates** and **Steve Balmer**, **Siegfried** and **Roy**, and **Ben** and **Jerry**, the ice cream boys. **Ben Cohen** told me he and Jerry really gelled because they had opposite strengths: "Jerry is good at production and much more logical, and I'm the creative end of it. Jerry was doing production, and I was doing sales and marketing. He had no desire to do what I was doing, and I had no desire to do what he was doing."

So, find somebody who's good at what you aren't and vice versa. Then focus like crazy on your strengths. Now excuse me while I go and focus on my real strength – consuming enormous quantities of Ben and Jerry's ice cream.

> **I think in order to be successful you have to surround yourself with people who can take care of your weaknesses.**
>
> **Wayne Schuurman** *president, Audio Advisor*

> **My great success has been because my partner was the wine maker and I'm the marketing and money guy. We had different strengths. We're like black and white.**
>
> **Donald Ziraldo** *cofounder, Inniskillin Wines*

MY ONE-WORD BUSINESS PLAN

IMPROVE

Successful people have a desire to keep improving themselves and their work, and I guess I'm no exception. It really bothers me if I think something I do isn't good enough. I've rewritten every page of this book and redrawn every graphic dozens of times, trying to improve it. I'll spend hours digging through my database to find a quote that makes the point just a little better. There are people in my office whose job is to try and stop me from making changes. They keep saying, "It's good enough. Stop rewriting or we'll never get the book out." Sorry, I just can't stop myself.

I confess I haven't always had this overpowering desire to improve things and make them better. I remember one of my early assignments in college was to design a paper sculpture. Of course, I had more important things to do, like socialize, so I whipped off a quick design and left it on the professor's desk. In the back of my mind I knew it wasn't great, but I hoped it would squeak by. The next day, as I was passing by the display case that exhibited the best student work, I stopped dead in my tracks. There was my paper sculpture on display! As I stood there thinking, "Gee, maybe it's not so bad after all!" My classmates appeared, rolling on the floor with laughter. They'd swiped the key to the display case and placed my abysmal paper sculpture next to the really good work. I was humiliated, but it was a defining moment. I said to myself, "I'm never going to produce anything that bad again." The fear of ridicule is a great motivator.

From that moment on I really tried to do good work. And "work" is the operative word, because I had to work my butt off to push my projects from mediocre to good. But over time I gradually improved and when a competition came along to create a new type of trophy, it was my design that took first place. And this time my work really did make it into the display case.

Suddenly, I discovered some of the benefits of doing good work, like the internal satisfaction and sense of self-worth. There were also external rewards, like the guys who laughed at me before were now telling me what a great job I did. Suddenly I was getting some respect. I also found if you do good work, then work comes to you. Instead of begging for a summer job, I was offered one. So, let's see… When I did bad work I was ridiculed and laughed out of the room. When I did good work I got satisfaction, respect, pats on the back, credibility, a job, and money. Hey, I was sold on the value of always trying to improve and make things better.

From then on, improving myself, and my work, became my guiding light. Whatever I did I just kept trying to make it better. When I started my company, I had no big goals or visions. I didn't even have a business plan. Wait, that's not true. Here's my business plan in one word: IMPROVE. When clients gave us a project, we put all our energy into doing good work and constantly improving it. We figured if we did that, then things like success, awards, acknowledgement, and money would follow – and they did.

So I'd say, when you're sitting there drawing up the business plan for your own life, consider this word for the cover – IMPROVE.

8
TO BE
GREAT

1. **PASSION**

2. **WORK**

3. **FOCUS**

4. **PUSH**

5. **IDEAS**

6. **IMPROVE**

7. **SERVE**

8. **PERSIST**

7. SERVE

Great people SERVE others something of value. Success isn't just about "me." It means serving other people in some way. So be able to focus on others, put yourself in their shoes, see their perspective, and bend over backwards to deliver something that has value for them. In return, you'll get a rich life. It's also the route to riches, because serving others is how people actually achieve wealth. The better you serve other people, the higher you'll go yourself.

SERVE OTHERS

SOMETHING THEY VALUE

The seventh trait that makes people great is SERVE. In this book we've talked a lot about "You" – you finding your passion, you working hard, focusing, pushing yourself, and improving. Now it's time to shift gears. Instead of looking inward we need to look outward, because achieving success (and wealth) involves serving other people.

Here's the awful truth: People don't care about you. They only care about how you can fix their problems, fix their plumbing, fix their pain. Make them laugh, make them cry, or make their day. Make them thinner or make them a winner. Give them information or inspiration. Lend them a hand or lend them your ear. Fill their stomachs, fill their minds, fill their soul, or fill a void in their life. In other words, people only care that you serve them something that has value for them and helps them in some way.

The word Serve is often misunderstood. Maybe it's because servers in restaurants say, "Hi, my name's Bobby and I'm your server." Then every time you want something, Bobby can't be found. And when I say "serve," many people think I mean in a charity sense, for instance Mother Teresa serving the poor. Charity is important, but it's only one aspect of serving. As you'll see in this chapter, serving others is how people get rich.

What I mean by Serve is thinking about others, working on their behalf, and delivering something they want, need, or value, whether it's a service, a product, an experience, or a feeling. It's delivering the goods and coming through for other people. And no matter what field you're in, serving is a big key to success. Four Seasons Hotels founder **Issy Sharp** told me it was serving others that took him to the top: "Service was really what set the company on its course – the idea of acting more as a host, being friendly, accommodating, giving the customer service." **Norbert Frischkorn** built a successful audiovisual staging business by serving his clients well: "I believe in serving people. We're there to do a job for our clients."

Explorer **Chris Kilham** travels the world studying native uses of medicinal plants and he says, "This is all about serving. I'm out to serve humanity by delivering safe remedies that help them with their health issues. I'm out to serve the environment through efforts to protect it. And I'm out to serve indigenous, native people. I'm totally in a serve capacity. That's the whole deal. That's what drives me." It also drives award-winning author and performer **Eve Ensler**: "I think success is to really see your life as serving. Period. We're here to do nothing else. Nothing else interests me, personally."

As you'll see in this chapter, people succeed by serving others in some way, shape, or form. So the two questions are: 1. Who do you serve? 2. What do you serve that has value for them?

> **I offer a service, and that's to clothe people.**
> *Alexander McQueen renowned fashion designer*

> **I think I'm here to serve. I'm a messenger about communication, about ideas, and turning them into pop culture.**
> *Paula Silver president, Columbia Pictures Marketing*

WHO DO YOU SERVE?

SALESPEOPLE SERVE **CUSTOMERS**
DOCTORS SERVE **PATIENTS**
WRITERS SERVE **READERS**
ENTERTAINERS SERVE **AUDIENCES**
TEACHERS SERVE **STUDENTS**
ATHLETES SERVE **SPECTATORS**
ACTORS SERVE **DIRECTORS**
POLITICIANS SERVE **VOTERS**
PROFESSIONALS SERVE **CLIENTS**

Who do you serve? This is an important question, because success in any field means really knowing the people you serve. In business, success hinges on serving customers, which is why famous General Electric CEO **Jack Welch** said, "We want a company that focuses on nothing but serving customers."

Professionals such as accountants, lawyers, engineers, and architects serve clients. Architect **Susan Ruptash** says, "It's a collaborative effort with a client and serving the client is essential for us. If we're not giving the client what they think is appropriate and right, then even if we think it's the greatest idea in the world, we've failed."

Entertainers serve their audience. *The Simpsons* creator **Matt Groening** told me, "The important relationship is with the audience, the people who actually watch the show, and that's what I always keep in mind." The audience is also on **Barry Friedman's** mind. He's one half of the **Raspyni Brothers**, an amazing juggling and comedy act: "We just keep thinking, 'Is the show good for the audience? Are they having a good time, are they getting their money's worth?'" And that attitude ensures the audience will get their moneys worth.

NASA whiz **Dave Lavery** sends robots to Mars, but it's the taxpayers on Earth he serves: "I chose to work as a federal government employee for NASA, rather than as a contractor making much more money. I guess I have a desire to work for the common good, rather than a dollar figure." Dave told me the way he measures his own success is: "Have I helped deliver a quantum advance in knowledge to the American taxpayer?"

In reality, we all serve numerous clients and success means understanding all their needs. **Ronda Carnegie**, advertising director for *The New Yorker* magazine, says, "I serve the publisher of the magazine. Then I have to make sure that I live up to the readers' expectations. And I also serve all the advertisers and have to make them happy. So it's a lot of serving." Athletes serve their coaches and their fans. Olympian figure skater **Elizabeth Manley** said, "I didn't want to disappoint people. You want to bring home gold. You want to make them proud of you."

I always thought leaders were the ones being served by their followers, but **Gail Prowse**, a leader in nursing education, told me it's really the other way around: "As a leader I'm there to serve my group. It's up to me to tune in to what the group needs and help people fulfill their potential." Presidents of countries need to serve the voters, or next election they're out of a job. And the top dogs in companies, such as Microsoft's **Bill Gates**, need to serve their boards of directors, shareholders, employees, and ultimately their customers, or they'll be in the doghouse.

Serving is so important that some businesses actually call themselves "service" businesses. But let's face it, no matter who you are, if you want to succeed in life you need to think of yourself as being of service to somebody. Who do you serve?

If you're not serving the customer, you'd better be serving someone who is.
Karl Albrecht billionaire founder of Aldi supermarkets

To command is to serve, nothing more and nothing less.
André Malraux famous writer and politician

SERVE OTHERS **VALUE**

EXPERTISE
USEFULNESS
ENTERTAINMENT
UNDERSTANDING
INFORMATION
EXPERIENCE
HUMOR
HEALTH

Successful people serve other people something that has VALUE for them. So the question is: What value do you serve others?

EXPERTISE has value. **Martha Stewart** spent years becoming an expert on homemaking, and her expertise had high value for millions of women clamoring for tips to make a better home. Martha says, "I came to all these people with trusted information, useful information, valuable ideas and products."

UNDERSTANDING has value. **Harry Rosen** sells suits, but he says the value that built Harry Rosen Men's Clothing into a major retailer is understanding: "My personal formula for success is understanding the customer, being able to sense and communicate with each consumer, and show them clothing that's most appropriate." Mathematics professor **Arthur Benjamin** helps students understand math: "I get paid to explain math to people. I love doing it, and it has value for others. I'm lucky being in a society that places value on explaining math to people."

INFORMATION has value, and you don't have to be in the news and magazine industries to serve it. Optometrist **Jerry Hayes** was tired of repeating the same information over and over to patients, so he wrote it out and printed some brochures that he could give patients to read. Other optometrists started asking for the brochures and suddenly Jerry had a whole new business. He says, "I discovered something I could sell to my own peers that added value for them."

ENTERTAINMENT has value. People place high value on a good novel or thrilling movie that puts them on the edge of their seats, and even one that makes them cry. Somebody said to me, "**Danielle Steel** writes such trashy novels. I don't know why people read them." Well, they may not be everybody's cup of tea, but those novels are serving millions of people with entertainment they value, and that's why Danielle has sold more books than any other living author.

SOLVING PROBLEMS has value. Pest controllers solve people's mouse problems and dentists solve their mouth problems. Either way it has high value for people. (My apologies to pest controllers for lumping you in with dentists.)

Smart Wireless CEO **Nez Hallett III** says, "The real secret to business is unlocking value. Go look for the value you can offer. Be vigilant at finding it every day and unlocking it, because that's really your competitive edge." I would add that unlocking value is the key to success in any area, not just business. So don't think, "What am I getting out of this?" Instead think, "What value am I serving others?" The higher the value, the higher you'll go.

> **When you have something to offer people, and they look at you as being an expert in your field, all of a sudden you think, "I've got value."**
> *Ian Craig president of wireless solutions, Nortel*

> **If you can give value to people, then they'll give value back to you. You're creating something that they want and will use.**
> *Jerry Hayes optometrist, founder of Hayes Marketing*

> **Strive not to be a success, but rather to be of value.**
> *Albert Einstein world's most renowned physicist*

SERVING OTHERS WILL GIVE YOU

**HAPPINESS
SATISFACTION
APPRECIATION
CONTRIBUTION
ACKNOWLEDGEMENT**

A RICH LIFE

Serving others is one of the most important things we can do to succeed, but we live in a "Me, Me, Me" world. Many of us are more into serving ourselves than others, so why bother helping other people at all? There are a couple of reasons, and the first is: Serving others will give you a rich life.

Having a rich life means being appreciated. **William James**, the father of modern psychology, wrote, "The deepest principle of human nature is the craving to be appreciated." And the way to be appreciated is to serve others something they appreciate. Top real estate agent **Elli Davis** does a great job for her clients and they show her their appreciation: "I like people to be really pleased with what I'm doing. When someone brings you a pot of flowers and says, 'You did a really great job,' that's really nice. Or they write you a note and they're really happy."

Having a rich life means happiness. Physician **Charles H. Burr** once said, "Getters generally don't get happiness; givers get it." Dynamica founder **Daniel Schwartz** says, "Serving other people serves me well. The more that I'm proud of what I do in my community or the world, the happier I am. It adds meaning to my life." And **Lindsay Sharp**, director of 4 London museums, said to me, "The people who get the greatest pleasure out of life are those who believe that what they're doing is going to make a difference for other people, and it also helps them."

Missionary doctor **Albert Schweitzer** went as far as to say the only way to achieve happiness is by serving others: "I don't know what your destiny will be, but one thing I do know: the only ones among you who will be really happy are those who have sought and found how to serve."

Having a rich life means acknowledgement. I mean, being acknowledged beats being anonymous any day. We all want to feel that we matter in some way. **Sherwin Nuland**, clinical professor of surgery at Yale, says we form the image of ourselves by serving others: "It was a privilege to serve as a doctor. And serving is the greatest privilege of all, because it gives you a sense of yourself and a self-image to be able to do things for other people. The real rewards have to do with doing for others."

So, the great irony is that by serving others, we actually end up getting a whole bunch of stuff back ourselves, and it all adds up to a rich life. As poet **Ralph Waldo Emerson** said, "It is one of the most beautiful compensations of this life that no man can sincerely try to help another without helping himself."

> **I think the more you share and the more you put out there, the more comes back to you.**
> **Don Green** *cofounder, Roots clothing*

> **You can have everything in life you want, if you will just help enough other people get what they want.**
> **Zig Ziglar** *renowned speaker and author*

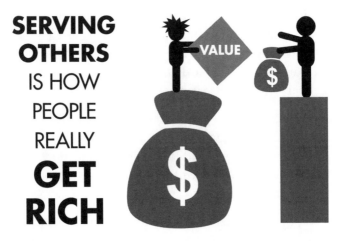

SERVING OTHERS IS HOW PEOPLE REALLY GET RICH

These days it seems like many people are more into serving themselves than serving others. So I figure I need to give you some additional motivation to want to serve other people. I mean, what's in it for you? We already talked about how serving others will bring you intangibles like happiness and a rich life. But maybe you're looking for something more tangible, something you can really get your hands around. Okay, how about a big bag of money? Because serving others is the way people really get rich.

Look at a list of billionaires and you'll see they got rich by serving others something of value, whether it's **Bill Gates** serving us software we want or **Sam Walton** serving us discounts at Wal-Mart. Some people become billionaires by serving low-cost products to many people. Ikea founder **Ingvar Kamprad**, serves well-designed, inexpensive furniture to millions of people. Others become billionaires by serving something that costs a lot, like **Michael Dell** and **Larry Ellison** who serve people high-priced computers and software that also has high value for them. **Martha Stewart** serves homemakers "useful information" and "valuable ideas" and that's what made her the first female self-made billionaire in America.

There's a myth that most people get rich by investing. I'm not saying they don't make some money that way, but it's a drop in the bucket compared to what they make by serving others. Only one of the top 10 billionaires got rich through investing – **Warren Buffett**. But unlike amateur investors trying to make money quickly in the stock market, investing is Warren's passion and business and he serves his investors a good return on their money. So he too got rich by serving others. The same goes for gambling. The ones who strike it rich through gambling are the people who own the casinos and serve the gamblers. I'm not saying don't invest or gamble, just don't expect to get rich that way. Most wealthy people invest, but after they're already rich and can afford to lose some. I invest, but it's like a hobby and I've lost a lot of money doing it. However, I've made a lot of money by serving people, just like so many other wealthy people.

The reality is you can become a millionaire in any field if you serve people well enough. There are millionaire plumbers, millionaire carpenters, millionaire dry-cleaners. You might be surprised to learn that the couple who run your local convenience store are millionaires. They didn't get rich by winning the lottery. They did it by serving people lottery tickets and food when every other store was closed. Oh, they don't look like millionaires. They drive beat-up cars and dress down, because if you knew they were millionaires you'd say, "I'm not shopping there. They're richer than me!"

I was discussing this with bestselling author **Seth Godin** and he agreed: "You don't become a millionaire without serving other people. I mean, we can whine all we want about Bill Gates, but if we didn't want what he gave us, he would have failed. The fact is, people who succeed are people who serve needs."

So take the time you'd spend investing or gambling and use it to serve others something they value. That's how you'll really become wealthy. Forget about striking it rich and think about serving it rich.

Strive to make something good that people want and the money will follow.
François Parenteau top independent Wall St. analyst

THE FORMULA TO GET RICH

1.
DO WHAT YOU **LOVE**

2.
SERVE OTHERS WHAT THEY LOVE

3.
GET **MONEY** IN RETURN

The Passion chapter said, "Do what you LOVE and the money will follow." That's true, but to make a lot of money you can't just do what you love – you also need to SERVE other people something they love. After all, it's other people who pay you money in return for something you serve them, and the more they love it, the more they're willing to pay. So here's the simple 3-step formula for achieving wealth:

LOVE + SERVE = MONEY. 1. Do what you love. 2. Serve others what they love. 3. Get money in return.

Bill Gates loved computers and software. But there are many people out there who love computers and they can barely pay the rent. The difference is Bill didn't just serve himself. He served software to others that they loved, or needed, and he got a lot of money in return – enough to make him the world's richest man. **Oprah** loves speaking, but there are many people who love to speak, even if they have nothing to say, and they're not rich. The difference is Oprah speaks about topics other people want to hear about and presents them in an entertaining way that people can relate to, and that's what made her a billionaire. **J.K. Rowling** started out with nothing except the passion to write. But she didn't write just for herself, she wrote for the Harry Potter in all of us. So kids love reading her books as much as she loves writing them, and that's what made her the richest woman in Britain.

Enough of the big names. The 3-step formula works for people in all walks of life. **Norbert Frischkorn** does the staging for corporate events like annual meetings and he says, "I love what I do and I'm in business to serve my clients a great event. If I do a good job they give me a big tip and then they come back again and give me more tips." The 3-step formula works in the medical profession where doctors earn a good living doing what they love and also serving us something we love – health! Surgeon **Douglas Dorner** said to me, "I still to this day love to get up in the morning and go do what I do. It is really gratifying. And society does value what we do for a living. Physicians and surgeons are well compensated."

I gave a summary of this book to a writer I know and after reading it he said to me, "I could never figure out why I'm not making more money from my writing, but now I know. I love writing and I'm doing everything you say leads to success, except for one thing – I'm not serving others; I'm just writing for myself." He was right. I could see he was passionately wrapped up in his subject, but it was a subject most people wouldn't be interested in, so why would they want to spend their hard-earned money on his book? I'm not saying everybody has to get rich. This writer is doing what he loves and getting a lot of satisfaction from it. But at the same time he feels there's something missing from his life – money!

So, follow the simple 3-step formula. Do what you love and also shape it into something others love. Then you'll achieve the best of both worlds – love and money.

> **Match what you love to do with what people want.**
> **Financial rewards are the by-product of that.**
> *Anthony Tjan senior partner, The Parthenon Group*

FORGET ABOUT YOURSELF

FOCUS ON THE PEOPLE YOU SERVE

Serving others leads to a rich life and riches. So the next few pages give some tips on how we can become better servers. The first way is to forget about yourself and focus on the people you serve.

Issy Sharp didn't build Four Seasons Hotels into one of the world's great hotel chains by thinking about himself. He told me, "You always have to give customers what they want, rather than doing what you want." Even when Issy is doing high-level negotiations, he focuses on the other person: "In any negotiation always, always, try to understand what the other person needs. I think you really have to be able to sit in the other chair and ask: How do I get that person what they need, as well as what I need?"

Whether it's a major hotel or a mini website, it pays to think of the person on the other end of the experience. Web design critic **Jakob Nielsen** says, "When people ask me for tips to design a good web site I say, 'Remember, you're not doing it for yourself. You're doing it for other people. What do other people think of it?'"

Of course, there are always going to be times when we go inward and dwell on ourselves. **Sam Sullivan** thought a lot about himself after a ski accident left him a quadriplegic. But it was when he started thinking of others that his own life turned around and he was elected mayor of Vancouver: "It's no longer just about me. I think, 'What can I do of value for other people?'"

Thinking of clients instead of himself has helped **Bob Rogers** and his company BRC Imagination Arts create some of the world's best visitor attractions for museums and theme parks. Bob told me one of the first questions he asks a client is: "What are you trying to accomplish? Never mind where I want to go. I want to get you to where you want to go."

But, wait a minute! Don't artists just paint for themselves? Well, one of the world's great realistic artists **Ken Danby** says, "That's crap. Artists try to communicate to others. How long would I paint if I was marooned alone on an island? I don't think I'd paint very long. My motivation would dissipate in a big hurry." Legendary music producer **Quincy Jones** puts it a little more bluntly: "Any artist who says, 'I'm gonna write and play what I want, and I don't care if anybody likes it,' is full of shit."

Yes, successful musicians like Quincy are out to serve their audiences, so that famous song "I Did It MY Way" should really be "I Did It THEIR Way." Come on, let's all sing our new theme song. I'll lead. Here goes: "I did it THEIR waaaaaay…" What's that? You'd rather sing alone! Okay, okay I can take a hint. My point is, if you want to succeed, it's better to be preoccupied with serving others, than me-occupied serving yourself.

> **I don't do a presentation on what I think. I do it on what the audience wants to know.**
> *John Caldwell* president & CEO, CAE

> **The best students I have are the ones who feel life is not about them. My most successful student doesn't worry much about himself.**
> *Douglas Jacobs* pastor and professor

PUT YOURSELF IN
OTHER PEOPLE'S SHOES

Success means focusing on the people you serve, and people have different ways of doing that. Some say, "Put yourself in other people's shoes," or "See the other person's perspective." It's also important to "Listen to the people you serve." On the next few pages are a little of each so you can see what works for you.

Let's start with "Put yourself in other people's shoes." **Nancye Green** told me, "Putting yourself in other people's shoes is the secret to life. I create solutions for other people, so I have to be able to get outside my skin and into theirs, or my solutions won't be successful." And being able to do that made Nancye's branding and marketing company Donovan/Green very successful.

When I asked Ben and Jerry's ice cream cofounder **Ben Cohen** what led to his success he said, "I think I'm good at being able to put myself in the shoes of my consumer." He might have said their stomachs, since Ben comes up with their ice cream flavors.

Four Seasons Hotels founder **Issy Sharp** told me he came up with many firsts by putting himself in his customers' shoes, and bathrobes: "There are dozens of things that we did, not because we thought as hotel managers, because we thought as customers. We were the first to put bathrobes in rooms, the first to put shampoo, bigger bars of soap, big soft towels, good showers. All these things were done as a result of thinking, 'This is what a customer might like.'"

When it comes to the medical profession, doctors are always poking around their patients' bodies, but surgeon **Douglas Dorner** told me you also have to put yourself in their shoes: "As a patient, you're sick, you're scared, you're frightened. As a surgeon, I think you have to put yourself in that patient's shoes and give them explanations they can understand. I think it's terribly important."

David Zussman, president of the Public Policy Forum, told me that putting yourself in other people's shoes isn't just a nice thing to do, it's critical to your success: "I know a lot of very smart people who have not made an impact, where others less talented have. I think, in large part, it's because the talented people are concentrating on themselves and success requires putting yourself in somebody else's shoes. I think successful people are always saying, 'Oh, yeah, I see where you're coming from.'" Grammy award-winning musician **Gary Burton** agrees: "I've known talented musicians who were not very good at putting themselves in other people's shoes and they did not become very successful."

So, success really depends on being able to put yourself in the shoes, loafers, high heels, sneakers, Birkenstocks, or Doc Martens of other people. Yeah, I know some shoes are really smelly so it can be kind of unpleasant. But if you don't do it your chances of success will really stink.

> **Even people you may violently disagree with, you stretch your mind to walk a little bit in their shoes and stand where they stand.**
> *Gerald Durnell CEO, ProTech Publishing*

> **Putting yourself in other people's shoes is highly underrated. In a service business like public relations you really have to put yourself in your client's shoes.**
> *Jessica Switzer president, Switzer Communications*

SEE THE OTHER PERSON'S PERSPECTIVE

Another way to become a better server is to see things from the other person's perspective. Journalist **Walt Mossberg** told me that's what helped him succeed at writing his popular technology column in *The Wall Street Journal*: "I can always put things in the perspective of a regular person. I imagine the reader to be a smart person who has neither the time nor interest to figure out the inner workings of these computers, but really wants to know." **Russell Campbell**, president of ABN AMRO Asset Management Canada, said, "Being sensitive to other people, I think, is my primary skill. You need to be able to relate to other people and see where they're coming from, then build a bridge between yourself and them."

Ian Craig, president of Nortel Networks wireless division, told me he puts everything in the perspective of his customer: "What's their measurement for the success of their business? Share price going up, number of new customers, or how quickly their network is up and running? Then I gear myself to making them successful." Sleep Country founder **Gord Lownds** said he takes the same approach in retail: "I always think from the customer's perspective and imagine what their experience is like. Then I try and construct something that makes it ideal for them and solves all of their problems."

Looking at it from the perspective of others doesn't just mean people. **Ian Miller** said one of the big reasons he won back-to-back World Cup show jumping titles is because: "You have to see life through the eyes of the horse. That's the real trick."

I don't know much about horses, but I once learned to see things from a cat's perspective. I was a junior assistant in a large photography studio and one of my assignments was to take a photo of a cat for a pet food package. I found the right cat and then dropped it in the middle of the huge photo studio, prepared to take the perfect shot. Except the cat took off like a shot. So there I was, frantically chasing this cat around the studio, crashing into lights and diving under tables trying to get a picture, like the coyote chasing the roadrunner. I was ready to shoot the cat with a gun instead of a camera, when one of the old pro photographers called me over and said, "Look at it from the cat's perspective." "Huh?" "If you were thrown into this strange environment with all the commotion, wouldn't you be jittery?"

So I got everyone out of the studio, made it dark and quiet, and put out a nice dish of cat food. Within a few minutes the cat nibbled the food, licked its paw, and I got a great shot. The moral of the story is if you don't want fur to fly, see the perspective from other's eyes.

> **View your own product with the customer's eyes.**
> *Jean Monty* chief executive officer, BCE

> **If there is one secret of success, it lies in the ability to get the other person's point of view, and see things from that person's angle, as well as from your own.**
> *Henry Ford* first person to mass-produce automobiles

LISTEN
TO THE PEOPLE YOU SERVE

If you want to be a better server, it pays to keep your ears open and listen to the people you serve. Ears are very important but mouths make more noise so everybody thinks they're the critical thing. However, successful people will tell you it's more important to have big ears than a big mouth. When I asked **Linda Keeler** what helped her become general manager of Sony Pictures she said, "I kept my mouth shut and my ears open and I listened." **Elliot Wahle** told me listening helped him become VP and general manager of Toys 'R' Us, Times Square: "My specialty is that I'm a good listener. It's an acquired skill. My dad once told me, 'The good Lord blessed you with 2 ears and 1 mouth, so listen twice as much as you speak.'"

Even people who may appear to have big mouths stress the importance of listening. Lawyer **Peter Silverberg** says, "A lot of people may think that a lawyer has to be good at talking, but I think listening is a really important facet of being a lawyer. It takes a lot of effort and a lot of concentration." I used to think that people in sales had to be big talkers, but top real estate agent **Elli Davis** told me, "You just listen. Keep your mouth shut and listen." BCE chief executive **Jean Monty** said, "If you go into a monologue with a customer, you won't make many sales. Go to a customer and listen to their needs, and then say, 'Okay, here's how my product will satisfy your needs.' So empathy and listening are basic skills of sales." Cisco Systems VP **Rick Moran** adds, "Customers usually tell you what they want if you listen hard enough."

Listening is so important there's a whole profession of people who get paid just to listen. They're called psychiatrists. They're also known as "shrinks" because that's what happens to your wallet after they listen to you. But, in a sense, we're all professional listeners, because no matter what field we're in, it really pays to tune-in to the people we serve. As Audio Advisor **Wayne Schuurman** says, "Listen to your customers or you go out of business."

The opposite is also true. Listen to your customers and you get more business. I mean, my company won a million-dollar contract because we listened. We were asked to do a proposal for a product launch and our client said, "Tell us how you'll handle the launch, but don't give us any creative ideas yet." We were tempted to do some zippy creative anyway, fearing our competitors would do it and win. But we listened to our client and gave him no creative. When he called with his decision he said, "You were the only ones who listened. So congratulations, you win the contract."

Many people don't listen, because it's hard work. I was reminded of this the other night at dinner when my wife blurted out, "You're not listening!" I shot back, "Hey, I'm a professional who has mastered the art of listening through hundreds of interviews." She responded, "Okay, tell me what I just said." My mind was blank. After spending all day listening to clients, I just couldn't stay tuned anymore. It really does take a lot of effort to listen, but not nearly as much effort as trying to make up with your spouse for not listening. Take it from me – it pays to listen.

> **We provide a technical service but what gives us an edge is listening. You need to understand what people really want rather than what you think they want.**
> *Paul Bunt* founder, Bunt and Associates Engineering

> **I would say that listening to the other person's emotions may be the most important thing I've learned in 20 years of business.**
> *Heath Herber* founder, Herber Company

BIG EGO MAKES A POOR SERVER

Another way to be a better server is to be able to set your ego aside. Now, I'm not saying ego is all bad. Ego is good in the sense that it says, "Hey, I can do this." But a big ego makes a poor server, because it's all about serving yourself, not others.

There's a myth that successful people have big egos. I can't say if they do or don't since I haven't measured them. But I can tell you this: Great people have the ability to set their egos aside. I've talked to over 500 very successful people, and I haven't seen a single visible display of ego. No arrogance, no boasting, even with those who have every right to toot their own horn. It's almost like the bigger the name the smaller the ego. I should say "apparent" ego because it could be really big, they just don't show it. And they seem to be more concerned about helping others than themselves. A few examples:

I saw **Quincy Jones** walking across a hotel lobby. Legendary music composer, winner of 26 Grammy Awards, and suddenly I had a chance to talk to him! I rushed over and said, "Quincy, can I get an interview?" His handlers quickly stepped in: "Sorry, Mr. Jones can't speak with you right now." Then Quincy butted in: "Wait a minute. I want to talk to this guy." And he sat down with me for 20 minutes while his handlers paced back and forth, because he probably had to be somewhere more important.

Another time I was standing with Hollywood legend **Norman Lear**, creator of great TV shows like *All in the Family* and *The Jeffersons*. He was in his 70's, a lot older than me, but he rushed away and brought back a chair to make me more comfortable. He didn't seem to care about his own comfort.

During coffee break at a conference, my colleague Thom and I were standing around surveying the crowd when he said to me, "Aren't you gonna interview Martha?" I looked up and there was **Martha Stewart** standing right in front of me, but I didn't recognize her because she didn't look like the TV Martha; no fancy makeup, clothes, or entourage, just Martha by herself talking on her cell phone. I'd heard she was tough so I was nervous, but I pushed myself to go up to her and ask, "Can I get an interview?" She put the cell phone down and said, "Of course, what would you like to know?" No third degree like, "Who are you?" or "Who's your publisher?" Those are the first questions I'm usually asked when I try to go through a public relations department to get an interview, and since I'm not a famous journalist writing for *Time Magazine*, they don't give me the time of day. I always get rejected. But if I can get to the big names themselves they usually say, "Sure, how can I help?"

The moral of the story is there's a myth that nice guys finish last, but from my experience I'd say nice guys finish first. And a lot of it has to do with being able to put their egos aside and serve other people in many little ways.

You want to make sure that your ego doesn't get in the way of your own success.

Joseph MacInnis physician, deep-sea explorer, author

BEND OVER BACKWARDS
TO HELP THE PEOPLE YOU SERVE

The last tip to be a better server is to bend over backwards to help the people you serve. Oreck Vacuum Cleaner founder **David Oreck** says, "We bend over backwards...If you're not delighted with what you get, we're going to make it right. We'll fix it, change it, or give you your money back. We'll even go out and wash your car if it'll help!"

Robin Budd directs great animated films where his characters can bend in just about any direction and he too will bend over backwards to help his clients, like Disney, create great films: "I serve the client and the client's problem, and to do that I will put myself out. I'll go without sleep. I'll be away from my family." Robin is typical of successful people who often put the needs of the people they serve ahead of their own. Four Seasons Hotels founder **Issy Sharp** told me, "You always have to give customers what they want, rather than being an artist who does what you want." And renowned architect **Jack Diamond** put it a little more bluntly: "We bust our ass for our clients."

Personally, I'm not a very flexible person. I can't even touch my toes. But I will bend over backwards and do whatever it takes to serve my clients. One of the big factors that has helped my company succeed for over 25 years is being willing to focus all our energy on helping clients, rather than spending a lot of time on ourselves. Clients always come first, we come second, and we'll do just about anything to help them succeed – put our personal lives on hold, cancel vacations, forget sleep, and even forget personal hygiene.

One example is when my company was producing a huge product launch. Colleague Thom Rockliff and I were working out of town and staying in a hotel, except we were so focused on our client's project we never went back to the hotel. We'd just flop down on the client's office floor and sleep for 20 minutes in the middle of the night, then get back up and keep working. This went on for days, and I started to notice that people in the office were holding their noses when they came around me. I figured I'd better clean up, so I went back to the hotel, tried my room key, and it didn't work. So I went to the front desk and they said, "Oh, sorry, we cleaned out your room. We thought you were dead." I said, "Look, I'm alive. I just smell like I'm dead." Thom would ship his clothes by FedEx to his mother, she'd wash them, and ship them back, so at least he was clean.

We were so intent on making the project successful we didn't want to spend a minute on ourselves. But the interesting thing is, by forgetting about ourselves and focusing 100% on making our clients successful, we, too, became successful. I also discovered something else: The people you serve don't care if you stink, as long as what you serve them doesn't.

> **I drive myself crazy over the needs of our clients.**
> **I care about the quality of our service.**
> *Jessica Switzer* president, *Switzer Communications*

> **You have to be willing to break your neck**
> **for customers. Once you do that, they do the**
> **same for you.**
> *Nez Hallett III* CEO, *Smart Wireless*

1. **PASSION**

2. **WORK**

3. **FOCUS**

4. **PUSH**

5. **IDEAS**

6. **IMPROVE**

7. **SERVE**

8. **PERSIST**

8. PERSIST

Great people PERSIST. There's no overnight success, so we need to persist through the years it takes to become great at anything. We also need to persist through mistakes and failures. And we need to persist through CRAP, which stands for Criticism, Rejection, Adversity, and Prejudice. Persistence is all about hangin' in there, taking small steps, not giving up, not looking back, and relentlessly moving forward.

BE PERSISTENT

The eighth trait that makes people great is PERSIST. The *8 To Be Great* are not in any particular order, since they're all important. But I thought it would be appropriate to make the Persist chapter the last one, because persistence is all about lasting. **James Baker**, CEO of the FX Palo Alto Laboratory, says, "The head of one of our divisions once told me the only reason he was in his job was just that he outlasted everyone else. Persistence counts for an awful lot."

Persistence must be important because we have so many words for it – Perseverance, Tenacity, Endurance, Stamina, Determination, Stick to It, and Hang in There, to name a few. **Louis Pasteur**, the great scientist who discovered the germ theory of disease, preferred to use the word tenacity. He said, "Let me tell you the secret that has led to my goal. My strength lies solely in my tenacity."

No matter what we call it, Persist means the ability to keep going through failure, pain, rejection, criticism, negativity, and crap – not to mention all the bad things we encounter. Universal Studios senior VP of design **Robert Ward** told me, "You really have to be prepared to persist because it won't be easy and there will be failure. You need to pick yourself up, stay on course and continue down that path."

The most successful people are often the most persistent people. Emmy Award-winning news anchor **Forrest Sawyer** says, "I have persistence to a fault. My friends say I'm like a dog with a bone. I get smacked in the nose and I just keep plugging along, and plugging along, and eventually it works." Greenpeace cofounder **Robert Hunter** told me he discovered the importance of persistence in one of his first jobs, as a traveling salesman selling encyclopedias door-to-door: "You had to be persistent because 50 doors would slam, but the 51st would open. I'd say that helped me doing journalism more than anything I was taught."

This chapter is the last of the 8-Traits, which means you're probably tired of reading. It's also the longest chapter in the book, so just when you want to cozy up to a nice easy little chapter, you get this huge one you have to slog through. Ha! Isn't that just so appropriate, that you have to PERSIST through the Persist chapter? Well, just do what so many successful people do and hang in there, stick to it, keep going, and do not give up. Think of this chapter as persistence practice for the real world.

It's being determined to persist. Being prepared to want to get there, regardless of the obstacles, and however difficult things seem.
Ann Turner founder, Profile Recruitment Consultants

I think one trait for success is perseverance. You just keep going at it and being tenacious. Don't let stumbling blocks get in the way. Try to learn from them, and not get defeated by them.
Steve Davis CEO, Corbis

PERSIST THROUGH
TIME

SUCCESS TAKES 10 YEARS

In this age of instant gratification, success is something that's very gratifying but far from instant. Achieving anything great never comes easily or quickly, which means a big thing we need to persist through is time. I don't know how to break this to you gently, so I'll just say it. Success takes 10 years. Sorry! I know a decade seems like an eternity, but that number 10 just keeps showing up in my research.

Famous modern dance choreographer **Martha Graham** said it takes 10 years to make a dancer. One study said it takes an average of 10.2 years for running champions to develop. (I've been at it for 30 years and I'm still waiting for the championship part.) **Ken Bradshaw** holds the world record for surfing the largest wave and he says it takes at least 10 years for a surfer to be able to ride those monster waves we see on TV. Surgeon **Douglas Dorner** told me it took "10 years plus an additional year of vascular surgery training before I could hang out my shingle." (After all that time, you'd think they'd give him aluminum siding instead of a shingle.)

In addition to careers, the 10-year journey also applies to many projects. **Albert Einstein** took 10 years to publish his Theory of Relativity. Microsoft CEO **Steve Ballmer** said it took Microsoft almost 10 years to get a successful version of Windows. **Steven Spielberg** had the rights to *Schindler's List* for 10 years before he felt ready to make the movie that won him the Oscar for Best Director. It took 10 years to develop the BlackBerry and 10 years to make the Google search engine successful. Google cofounder **Larry Page** told me, "It takes a long time to do these things and you need to be pretty single-minded."

Before starting my own company, I worked at a big corporation for 10 years. Actually, I left a month before getting my 10-year company pin. But that decade of experience was the foundation for my success, so I ended up getting something much better than a pin. I earned a membership in the "10-Year Success Club."

Yes, success takes time. I'm not telling you this to depress you. I'm doing it so you won't get depressed when you think you'll whip something off in a few months and years later you're still working on it. Now when that happens you can say, "Oh yeah, there's that 10-year thing," and by then you'll be so far down the road you won't want to quit. You'll just hang in there, keep going, and wake up one day to realize that you too are a member of the "10-Year Success Club."

> **For the first 10 years they called us the small people, the fly-by-night. And all the people who used to say those things about us are now gone. It took 10 years to build it up.**
> *Nez Hallett III CEO, Smart Wireless*

> **Success for me was spending over a decade in complete obscurity… My writing time was ten at night until three in the morning. I did that for over 10 years.**
> *David Baldacci bestselling fiction writer*

THERE'S NO OVERNIGHT SUCCESS

The Loch Ness Monster, Bigfoot, UFO's – these are all things people claim to have seen, but there's not much evidence they exist. In the interests of science, I would like to add one more to the list: The Overnight Success. In my own research of more than 500 people, plus combing through thousands of other success stories, I have yet to find a single example of true overnight success.

Dawn Lepore is a very successful Chief Information Officer at Charles Schwab, and she said, "Success did not happen overnight for me. I had to work very, very hard. It was not overnight." Chiat/Day advertising cofounder **Jay Chiat** said, "I started the agency when I was 29 and I worked for somebody else before that. So it took awhile, and it was a big awhile. It was an overnight success we spent 15 years working on."

Oh, sure, some people appear to rush to the top. **Christina Aguilera** was 8 when she sang the National Anthem before an audience of 50,000 people, but it wasn't until a decade later, at 18, that she became well known. Other singers such as **Britney Spears** and **Celine Dion** have similar stories. The myth of overnight success is nothing new. **Mozart** was 6 when he had his first public appearance, so we think he was an overnight success, but it took him another 10 years before he produced an acknowledged masterpiece.

So, when you see those kids on TV who seem to be overnight successes, don't forget that on the road to success they got their beginners permits when they were still in diapers. Golf superstar **Tiger Woods** says, "I started when I was about nine months. Yeah, just hopped out of my walker, and I was swinging." If you started on something when you were 9-months old, and worked on it every day like Tiger, then 10 years later you'd be pretty good at it too.

At one point I thought I'd found one example of real overnight success. **Sky Dayton** was quite young when he started EarthLink and sold it for a gazillion dollars, so the first thing I said to him was, "Sky, you're an overnight success…" But he quickly corrected me: "EarthLink didn't happen instantly. Before that I had a window washing business, a candy store, a couple of coffee houses, a computer graphics company. It was baby steps." Actor/ singer **Jennifer Lopez** sums it up when she says, "It hasn't been overnight. There's no such thing as overnight in this business." (Although in Hollywood there is overnight marriage.)

So, I'm still on the search for the elusive Overnight Success. If you find one, send over a photo and I'll put it in my display case, along with those blurry photos of the Loch Ness Monster, Bigfoot, UFO's, and the teenager who actually listened to his parents.

> **In the beginning, I was chief cook and bottle washer, a one-man sales force…Now, 41 years later, we're an "overnight success." Actually, it's what happens with a lot of hard work.**
> *David Oreck founder, Oreck Vacuum Cleaners*

> **It doesn't happen instantly and I think people need to realize that. Don't be discouraged just because it takes awhile. Realize there are steps, so you may not get there right away.**
> *David Carson renowned graphic designer*

PERSIST
THROUGH
FAILURE

It would be nice if there were "Failure Ahead" signs on the road to success. Then we'd know what was coming and could avoid it. But life's not like that. So we're cruising along just fine, heading towards success and suddenly – Yeow! – the road drops, we plunge straight down a steep hill, and end up splattered against a sign that reads "Welcome to Failure." In spite of the efforts of the Failure Marketing Board to improve its image, it's still a place nobody wants to visit. But all successful people do fail, and if you want to succeed, you'll probably end up there too. As doctor and deep-sea explorer **Joseph MacInnis** says, "Failures are just a kind of road map. Everybody who is successful looks at a trail of failures. It's part of the deal."

Just about every successful person I talked to said they failed in one way or another, and that also goes for people I didn't talk to. **Abraham Lincoln** failed in business twice, had a nervous breakdown and was defeated in politics 8 times. He kept persisting and ended up President of the United States. **Einstein**, the world's most famous scientist, failed an exam that would have allowed him to study for a diploma as an electrical engineer. The great painter **Paul Gauguin** died penniless. **Winston Churchill** failed grammar in primary school, plus his army entrance exam, not once, but twice, and still became the great British Prime Minister. No wonder he said, "Success is the ability to go from failure to failure without losing your enthusiasm."

François Parenteau told me that when he started in the investment business: "I did pretty bad initially. I did about as good as a skydiver who jumps out of the plane and forgets to strap on his parachute. So, I came crashing down." But François picked himself up, and has since been named top independent analyst by *Business Week*. **Lance Armstrong** also came crashing down when he started cycling: "I came in dead last in the field of 111 riders. I crossed the finish line almost a half-hour behind the winner, and as I churned up the last hill, the Spanish crowd began to laugh and hiss at me." They stopped hissing when Lance started winning back-to-back world championships.

Of course, nobody wakes up in the morning and says, "I think I'll fail today." But when it happens, the trick is to just keep going and persist through it. Direct marketing guru **Joseph Sugarman** said, "I failed at practically everything I tried, but I never gave up. I just knew that one of these days I'd make it if I just hung in there."

So, when you slide downhill into the town of Failure, pick yourself up, get out of town and keep going. Don't think of failure as the end of the road. Think of it as a little detour on your way to a much better place called Success.

> **I failed my way right to the top.**
> *Paul Haggis Academy Award-winning filmmaker*

> **Failing doesn't stop you. Quitting stops you. Persevere and don't be afraid to fail. You can afford to fail over and over again, because there will always be many, many more opportunities to succeed.**
> *Gerry Schwartz chief executive, Onex*

MAKE **FAILURE** YOUR **SCHOOL**

NOT YOUR **FUNERAL**

Failure can be heartbreaking, and when it happens you have a choice. You can let it be your school or your funeral. It's your school if learn from it and move on. It's your funeral if you become devastated and let it stop you in your tracks. Even if you don't like school, it beats a funeral any day, and that's why so many successful people try to look at failure as a learning experience.

Ben Saunders became the youngest person to ski solo to the North Pole, but he told me his first try was a disaster: "My first expedition was, in so many ways, the biggest failure of my entire life. We didn't get anywhere near the Pole and came back in massive debt. I was mentally ruined and convinced that I'd failed. But if I hadn't gone through that first expedition, I wouldn't be where I am now. So replace the word failure with learning – that's what it's all about."

David Fairchild said, "Don't look down on failure. I have learned many fascinating things by my failures, things which are as interesting as the successes." Since David was a world-famous botanist (I feel a pun coming on), he actually flowered from failure (sorry). Moving from botany to technology, Cisco Systems' **Rick Moran** says, "You learn something from failure. If you go into something that you thought you could do and you find out that you can't, learn a little bit about it, forgive yourself for having done it, and get the hell out."

Movies often fail at the box office, but animation film director **Robin Budd** says the learning still pays off: "You can't get too hung up about failures because they teach you many things. Failure is something that I am terribly afraid of, but it is a big part of the whole process." Comedian **Sinbad** adds: "Enjoy the fall off the horse. Enjoy the not being able to drive a car or the fact that you're not that good with a camera yet. That's when you learn the most." Creativity expert and author **Roger von Oech** says failure has a couple of benefits: "First, if you do fail, you learn what doesn't work; and second, the failure gives you the opportunity to try a new approach."

Yes, as much as we hate failure, it can be a much better school than success. Sure, success feels good, but when we succeed we just say, "Wow!" It's only when we fail that we ask, "Why?" Bell Mobility chairman **Bob Ferchat** says, "Successes reward you and pat you on the back, but they don't really teach you very much. Failure is where you learn, and understand why it happened, and what you did wrong. Successes are just rewards for continuing to fail."

So, if you're feeling really down from all the failures and flubs you're making, think of them as your school, not your funeral. Don't crash and burn - crash and learn.

> **You want failure to be an opportunity to learn and not a block to your forward motion.**
> *Bruce Cockburn singer, songwriter*

> **The times I have experienced failure have been the most growing for me, had the most important impact. Success is wonderful but failure is when you really meet yourself and ask, "Who am I?"**
> *Cynthia Trudell first woman to run a U.S. auto company*

TO SUCCEED A LOT
FAIL A LOT

To succeed a lot, it helps to fail a lot. So if you're not as successful as you'd like to be, maybe you're just not failing enough. Remember that **Babe Ruth** had the most success in terms of home runs, but he also had the most failures in terms of strikeouts. There are many other examples that show quantity counts – the more times you fail, the more times you can succeed.

Rower **Silken Laumann** says that when she started rowing she tipped the boat over more than anyone else: "The first time I started rowing I tipped 21 times. Just to put it in perspective, most people tip maybe once or twice in their entire career. This is how my summer went: Splash! Crawl back into the boat. Splash! Crawl back into the boat. Splash! Crawl back into the boat." Yet all those failures helped turn Silken into a world-champion rower. Moving from sports to science, **Albert Einstein** once said, "Ninety-nine times the conclusion is false. The hundredth time I am right."

It's almost like successful people collect "Frequent Failure Points" – sort of like Frequent Flyer Points, where the more you fly, the more points you get towards a free ticket. With Frequent Failure Points, the more you fail, the more points you get towards success.

Real estate agent **Elli Davis** has lots of Frequent Failure Points. She says, "I was going through old files the other day and I can't tell you how many times I did not get the deal. People say, 'Oh, Elli, she gets everything!' And I say, 'You should see what I don't get.' It's a numbers game. I get a lot because I do a lot." And that helped take Elli to the top of her profession.

Google cofounder **Sergey Brin** said to me, "You have to fail many times to succeed once." When he said that, my immediate response was, "Wait a minute, Sergey! Google isn't exactly a failure. It's a super colossal success," to which he responded, "Google didn't fail, but we have many projects that do fail. Not all projects work out." It's comforting to know that even the big guys rack up their share of Frequent Failure Points, the same as we little guys.

In my company, we learned long ago that to succeed a lot you've got to fail a lot, so when we're trying to come up with ideas for an ad campaign, a video, or even where to have lunch, we'll generate dozens of ideas. All of them will fail and get tossed in the garbage, except for one. And that's okay, because one good idea is all we need.

So if you'd like to have more successes, have more failures. Start earning your own Frequent Failure Points today. They could be your ticket to success.

I've missed more than 9,000 shots in my career. I've lost almost 300 games...I've failed over and over and over again in my life. And that is why I succeed.
Michael Jordan basketball superstar

I believe in a lot of failures, and failing quickly. That way you don't spend too much money, waste too much time, and you can move on to the next thing.
Russell Campbell president, ABN AMRO Canada

PERSIST THROUGH MISTAKES

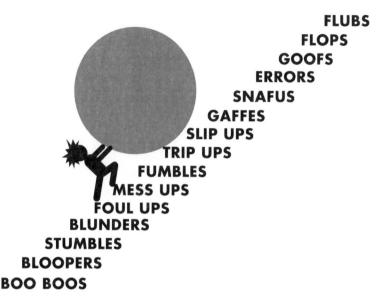

FLUBS
FLOPS
GOOFS
ERRORS
SNAFUS
GAFFES
SLIP UPS
TRIP UPS
FUMBLES
MESS UPS
FOUL UPS
BLUNDERS
STUMBLES
BLOOPERS
BOO BOOS

At first, I was going to lump mistakes in with failures, since mistakes are sort of mini-failures. However, I figured they really deserve their own section because so many successful people say they continually make flubs, errors, boo boos, blunders, bloopers, goofs, gaffes, and snafus; they muck up, mess up, slip up, trip up, and foul up; not to mention flop, fumble, and stumble. But they just keep persisting through it all.

Kevin Eubank, "Mississippi Parent of the Year" and construction firm owner, told me, "Everyone makes mistakes. It's how you handle those mistakes. Those that learn from their mistakes are the ones who are the most successful. Those that don't learn are the ones that are not in business anymore." Great corporate management guru **Peter Drucker** said, "You don't learn things out of books, you learn things by getting your hands dirty. You learn things by making the stupid mistakes." (I've tried to make smart mistakes, but they don't seem to be any better.) Actually, if you're making a lot of stupid mistakes, it could be a sign you're on your way to success. As actor **Joan Collins** once said, "Show me a person who has never made a mistake and I'll show you somebody who has never achieved much."

The good thing about mistakes is they often open up new possibilities, which is why renowned jazz innovator **Ornette Coleman** said, "It was when I found out I could make mistakes that I knew I was on to something." Umbra cofounder **Paul Rowan** told me mistakes helped his company become a leader in the design of contemporary products for the home: "People always talk about their successes, but I talk about how I made mistakes and turned them into success. When you're doing innovative products, you're going places that people haven't gone before, so you're bound to make some mistakes along the way. That's really the key to our success."

Famous philosopher **Daniel Dennett** said to me, "Make more mistakes, make better mistakes, more sophisticated mistakes. Be willing to make mistakes in public and admit them. Try to get over your embarrassment and your anger and your shame, and instead adopt an attitude of curiosity about your own mistakes." (I can see this one's gonna take a lot of practice.)

The thing is, each wrong way leads us to the right way, so each mistake is like a compass, but instead of pointing to true north, it's pointing us towards true success. So if you're not achieving the success you want, maybe you need to make more boo boos, blunders, and bloopers. How many mistakes have you made today? Sorry, that's not enough.

> **There are days when I've made the same mistake 14 times, and I say, 'Do I have any sense?'**
> *Oprah Winfrey top talk show host*

> **I hope you understand that business is a series of trial-and-error. It's not a great science. Mistakes are made. It's just moving the ball forward.**
> *Jack Welch CEO, General Electric*

DEVELOP A **CRITICISM FILTER** IN YOUR HEAD

On the road to success we have to persist through a lot of **CRAP** – **Criticism**, **Rejection**, **Adversity**, and **Prejudice**. These are all factors we have little control over and we just have to persist through them.

CRITICISM is a big one, and it's not usually something we look forward to. To persist through the criticism, it helps to remember that throughout history some of the most successful people have also been the most criticized. The great composer **Mozart** had to put up with criticism from **Emperor Ferdinand**: "Far too noisy, my dear Mozart. Far too many notes." Even **The Beatles** were roundly criticized by Decca Records: "We don't like their sound, and guitar music is on the way out." So if you're being criticized, congratulations! You could be on your way to success. The trick is to hang in there through criticism and not let it destroy you. It should be the critics who are destroyed, not you. Award-winning author and performer **Eve Ensler** said to me, "In spite of bad reviews, in spite of people attacking you for your beliefs, you just have to get up every morning and keep going."

In order to keep going, many successful people seem to develop a CRITICISM FILTER in their heads that has 2 functions: **1. Deflect Destructive Criticism.** If somebody says something that's just a put-down and doesn't help you at all, then your criticism filter deflects it, sending it in one ear and out the other, bypassing sensitive parts of your head such as tear glands.

Comedian and satirist **Rick Mercer** developed a strong Criticism Filter that helped him ignore all the flak encountered in show business. He said to me, "I've had some brutal, brutal criticism. When I did my first one-man show, a critic said on the radio, 'Dear Rick Mercer, you should never set foot on the stage again. Your show is an abysmal disaster.' He just ripped me apart. Luckily, I was 18 and very cheeky, so it didn't affect me. It could have easily driven other people from the stage, and they would never go back."

2. Accept Constructive Criticism. The other important function of our criticism filter is to accept constructive criticism. So if somebody says something that can help, we use it to improve. It was accepting criticism that led to **James Watson** and **Francis Crick** making their big discovery of the structure of DNA. James told me that when he showed their model of DNA structure to a chemist, he criticized it: "He said, 'It's wrong, you've got the hydrogen atoms in the wrong place.' I'd just put them down like they were in the books." James could have ignored the criticism, but he accepted it: "The next day, I thought he might be right, so I changed locations [of the atoms] and we knew we were right. It all happened in about 2 hours, from nothing to Bing! And we knew it was big." Big is an understatement, since it won James and Francis the Nobel Prize.

So develop your own Criticism Filter that deflects destructive criticism and accepts constructive criticism. Make it part of your own DNA and it could lead you to a really big "Bing!"

> **Sometimes the criticism is correct. Sometimes you need to say, "Maybe I am wrong and I need to course correct here."**
> *Lise Buyer renowned Wall Street investment banker*

> **If you give me constructive criticism, I'll make the change right away. But if you're just negative for the sake of being negative, I don't want to hear about it.**
> *Steven Schwartz author, "How to Make Hot Cold Calls"*

WARNING!
FRANK CRITICISM

People don't always have time to stop and think about how to make their criticism sound constructive, even if it is. That's why some guy named Frank invented "Frank Criticism," which gets right to the point without being nice. You may encounter Frank Criticism in the business world because people are often in a hurry, with a lot on their minds, like where to eat lunch, so they don't always have time to phrase things nicely. Once when General Electric CEO **Jack Welch** was critiquing a storyboard from their ad agency, he simply threw it on the floor and said, "We don't like it! It doesn't work!"

In spite of appearances, Frank Criticism is not always destructive. It's just the way it's presented that seems destructive. The criticism itself may actually be constructive and help us improve. **Terry Gilliam** told me it was Frank Criticism that helped the Monty Python group produce such wonderful TV shows: "The great thing about the group is that we were ruthless with each other. If an idea sucked, we said it sucked. We respected each other enough to do that. I know they say, 'Oh, make sure you don't put somebody down.' But put 'em down. People are incredibly strong and resilient. You want to encourage people, but if they're not producing good work, then you slap 'em."

188

I first discovered Frank Criticism in kindergarten when our teacher Mrs. Singer had us draw an outdoor scene and I drew a line across the top of the page to represent the sky. Another kid, probably named Frank, looked at my drawing and said, "Are you ever stupid. There's no line in the sky!" Good thing this kid wasn't in kindergarten with Picasso: "Hey, Picasso, you idiot, you gotta put the guy's nose on his face, not on his shoulder." At first I was hurt, but then I went outside and looked up, and realized, "Gee, he's right. There is no line in the sky." So he gave me new insight – and I gave him a black eye.

Now, fast forward to when I was in art college studying design. Professor Charlie had us design a new screwdriver and I spent weeks coming up with what I thought was the world's best design. Presentation day arrived, I rushed to class, and proudly placed my screwdriver on the judging table. Charlie walked along eyeing all the work – then suddenly he stopped and picked up my screwdriver. Yes! I was elated. He was obviously going to use my masterpiece as an example of breakthrough design – which, in a way, is what happened. Charlie hurled my precious screwdriver against the wall and it broke into a million pieces. I was devastated. I think my heart actually stopped. But, after I put a contract out on Charlie's life, I started thinking that maybe, just maybe, my design wasn't as brilliant as I thought it was. And I went away and designed a much better screwdriver.

I don't recommend the shatter approach to criticism. Simply saying, "It's not good enough, make it better," would have worked just fine. But I must admit that after watching Charlie shatter my screwdriver, there's not much any critic can say to shatter me – which was probably the point of the exercise.

The bottom line: It helps to get used to dealing with criticism. There are a lot of Franks and Charlies out there.

PERSIST THROUGH REJECTION

The "R" in CRAP stands for REJECTION. It's another thing successful people need to persist through and, no matter how you look at it, rejection is just a painful kick in the butt. And don't expect to be rejected only once. It's called re-jection because it happens repeatedly.

There's a long list of great people who were rejected over and over again and still achieved incredible success. **Ruth Handler** was rejected when executives at the Mattel toy company laughed at her idea for a doll. She persisted and created Barbie, the world's most popular doll. **Debbi Fields** had a great idea for cookies, but was rejected with these words: "A cookie store is a bad idea. Besides, the market research reports say America likes crispy cookies, not soft and chewy cookies like you make." Debbi persisted and ended up making a lot of dough.

It's hard to believe cyclist **Lance Armstrong** was ever rejected but he says, "No one wanted me. No European teams wanted me, and corporate America didn't want me." But they sure wanted him when he was winning the world championship year after year. Hotelier **Issy Sharp** told me he had the idea of building a new type of motor hotel, but he drove straight into rejection: "For years I knocked on doors and had flat-out rejection, with people saying, 'Kid, you don't know what you're talking about. You don't even know anything about the business. Why would you even think you can do it?' But that didn't deter me, because I just saw and felt something that I thought would work." Issy persisted and took Four Seasons Hotels to the top of the luxury hotel market.

Photojournalist **Rick Smolan** told me, "When I went to see publishers with the first *Day in the Life* idea, I got laughed out of every office." But the joke was on the publishers when Rick's *Day in the Life* books became bestsellers. Musician **Ed Robertson** told me the Barenaked Ladies experienced the same kind of rejection by big record labels: "We were rejected by all the record companies and told we would never get a record deal. But music made us really happy and we had fun doing it, so we just kept doing it." And they kept persisting to the top of the charts.

Psychiatrists listen to many tales of rejection, but it never occurred to me that they also get rejected, until psychiatrist **Ken Woodrow** said, "My professor, who was the chairman of the pre-medical panel of the college, said I didn't have what it took to be a good doctor and he would see to it that I never went to medical school. I cried." But Ken had the last laugh when he persisted and become a doctor and Professor of Psychiatry at Stanford.

So remember, when you get rejected, you're going to get dejected, but also get injected with the determination to persist. (Especially through cheesy rhymes.)

> **There'll be weeks when, boom, boom, boom, boom – 4 things get rejected. And you just think, "Well, the hell with this. I've got to get another job." It can get discouraging, but inevitably it turns around.**
> *Chip Kidd* acclaimed book cover designer

> **I think you have to develop a kind of resistance to rejection, and to the disappointments that are sure to come your way.**
> *Gregory Peck* celebrated film star

THINK OF **REJECTIONS** AS **BADGES OF HONOR**

Many successful people have an interesting strategy to persist through rejection. They treat their rejections like "Badges of Honor," sort of like war veterans wearing their medals. The rejection slips show what they've been through and act as a reminder to keep persisting.

This strategy helped bestselling novelist **Stephen King** persist when he first started writing. He was rejected over and over by publishers, but instead of throwing out the rejection slips, he pounded a nail in the wall above his bed and stuck them on it. He writes, "By the time I was fourteen...the nail in my wall would no longer support the weight of the rejection slips impaled upon it. I replaced the nail with a spike and went on writing." I love that story.

Many writers can tell you exactly how many rejection badges they have. **Seth Godin** told me, "When I got into the book business, I got 950 rejection letters before I sold my first book." **John Grisham's** first book was rejected by more than 30 publishers and 43 rejected the first "Dr. Seuss" book. All these writers stuck to it and became bestselling authors.

Some people frame their rejection slips and proudly display them for all to see. One lawyer-turned-writer was rejected by publishers hundreds of times. After he achieved great success he wallpapered the huge 20' by 20' bathroom in his mansion with all the rejection slips. Then he could sit there and laugh at all the people who said his writing was crap.

It's interesting that rejection actually seems to contribute to success in many cases. Maybe it pushes you to prove yourself or say, "I'll show them!" Music great **Quincy Jones** had his share of rejections and his wife Peggy Jones said, "I began to see this pattern time and time again in Quincy's life...with each rejection he'd come back stronger and stronger." Information architect **Richard Saul Wurman** says, "My wife claims I warm up only upon rejection...Rejection inspires me."

I wish I could say rejection inspires me, but usually it just tires me. To be honest, I've never been good with rejection, but I've gotten better thanks to the continual rejection I faced every time I asked people for an interview for this book. Most of the time people are happy to help, but I've also been flat-out rejected.

One rejection that stands out for me was **Matt Groening**, creator of *The Simpsons*. He rejected me, get this, 4 years in a row. Every year I'd see him at a conference and ask for an interview, and every year he'd refuse. But I kept asking, and finally he said yes. Matt gave me a great interview, and he also gave me my own personal drawing of Bart Simpson. It's hanging on the wall beside my desk, as a constant reminder that persistence really pays off.

> **I have 175 rejection slips in my files. I keep them around to remind me that if you give up at any point, nobody in the world cares that you're not succeeding, except you. So you have to really want it. You have to keep at it. And if you do, nobody can stop you.**
>
> **Robert J. Sawyer** *bestselling science fiction writer*

SOME **STRATEGIES** TO **PERSIST**

It's not easy to persist, so let's look at some Persistence Strategies that can help us hang in there and keep going. The first is to TAKE SMALL STEPS. Adobe Systems CEO **John Warnock** said to me, "One of the important things in life is to look down at your feet and take the next step and then the next step. Don't focus on things too far away, but make sure your direction is right and take one step at a time." Yes, we reach success in much the same way a baby learns to walk – by stumbling along and taking small steps.

Forrest Sawyer told me small steps took him from unknown radio announcer to famous TV news anchor: "I started with 1-minute pieces, and then I would do 3-minute pieces until I got them right. And then I did 10-minute and 13-minute pieces." Small steps took **Peter Cochrane** from a childhood of poverty to the chief technologist position at British Telecom: "I thought it would be wonderful if I could get a technician's qualification. Then I thought it would be wonderful if I got a Bachelor's degree. Then a Master's degree, then a Ph.D., then a D.Sc. One step at a time."

Alexander Tsiaras is CEO of Anatomical Travelogue, a pioneer in the field of medical-imaging technology, and he points out that many small steps can make it seem like you've taken a huge leap: "People say to me, 'Oh, you guys made a quantum leap from the technology you had last year.' I say, 'No, we didn't. Our algorithms got a little cleaner, CPU's got a little cheaper, memory a little bigger. If you add up the incremental advances in every one of them, it looks like you've made a quantum leap. But it's actually many small steps.'"

The great thing about small steps is they make it easier to get going in the first place. Famous writer **Mark Twain** once said, "The secret of getting ahead is getting started. The secret of getting started is breaking your complex overwhelming tasks into small manageable tasks, and then starting on the first one." It worked for **Graham Hawkes**, who holds the world record for the deepest solo ocean dive, and he also builds those cool submersibles that take divers to the bottom of the sea. It's complex technology, but Graham says small steps keep the problems from sinking him: "I build these submersibles and if I really understood how long, and how much money and effort it would take, I'd never start. Where's the money coming from? Will it work? Will people want it? So, you have to fool yourself into not looking at all the problems. Just focus on the next step."

Climbing the stairway to success is like climbing a mountain. There's no easy way up. Sorry, they haven't installed escalators yet. But taking small steps will help, and even though they're small, they can take you all the way to the stars. As astronaut **Neil Armstrong** said when he set foot on the moon, "That's one small step for man; one giant leap for mankind."

> **I've learned that if I just put one foot in front of the other, things will work out well. And I believe that.**
> *Gord Lownds* founder, Sleep Country

> **Life is hard by the yard, but by the inch it's a cinch.**
> *Quincy Jones* renowned music composer/producer

QUITOPHOBIA

> You're crazy.
> Pack it in!

> I don't quit!

There are a lot of fears out there. I mean, I just read a list of phobias, and there were the usual ones like Acrophobia (fear of heights) and my personal favorite, Ophidiophobia (fear of snakes). But would you believe there are over 500 other phobias? There's even Phobophobia (a fear of phobias). One poor little letter of the alphabet that doesn't seem to have a phobia is Q. So, in the name of science, I'd like to coin the first "Q" phobia – Quitophobia, an intense fear of quitting.

Many successful people have Quitophobia and that's a good thing, because it helps them persist. You can tell CNN founder **Ted Turner** has it when he says, "Why do you think my own racing yacht is named Tenacious?...Because I never quit. I've got a bunch of flags on my boat, but there ain't no white flags. I don't surrender. That's the story of my life." And refusing to quit helped Ted win the ultimate sailing trophy, the America's Cup.

Lance Armstrong has Quitophobia and it helped him win the ultimate cycling trophy, the Tour de France, 7 times. He picked up Quitophobia from his mother who always told him, "Son, you never quit." Early in his career, Lance was competing in a triathlon when he ran out of energy and was about to pack it in. His mother found him on the course and reminded him that he couldn't quit – so Lance walked to the finish line.

It's not that successful people don't think of quitting. **Ben Saunders** told me there were times when he wanted to quit during his 800-mile ski trek to the North Pole: "There was a white-out for days where I couldn't see anything, and that's the closest I came to going completely nuts. At times I would fall over and be disappointed that I hadn't fractured my wrist or broken my ankle, so I could get picked up and flown home with my pride intact." But Quitophobia kept Ben persisting and he became the youngest person to ski solo all the way to the North Pole.

We've talked a lot about sports, but great people in every field have Quitophobia You can tell star talk show host **Oprah Winfrey** has it when she says, "I couldn't bear to think of myself as a quitter." In technology, Sun Microsystems chief scientist **Bill Joy** has Quitophobia: "I'm tenacious. I don't give up just because it's hard. The important thing is the stick-to-it-ness, so hang in there."

All the evidence shows that if you want to reach success, then hanging in there and not quitting counts for a lot. So if you must have a phobia, I'd say forget heights, snakes, and the other 500 phobias, and go for Quitophobia.

Eventually you learn that the competition is against the little voice inside you that wants you to quit.
George Sheehan physician, author, runner

There's only one thing that can guarantee our failure, and that's if we quit.
Craig Breedlove 5-time land speed record holder

Age wrinkles the body. Quitting wrinkles the soul.
Douglas MacArthur famous World War II general

STRATEGIES TO PERSIST

NEVER NEVER

We just talked about Quitophobia – never quitting. I was going to leave it at that, but there are so many NEVER GIVE UP comments in my research, this persistence strategy deserves its own page.

During World War II, British Prime Minister **Winston Churchill** told the British people, "Never, never, never give up." And today successful people still rely on the same strategy. **Deana Brown**, CEO of Powerful Media, told me, "If I am successful, it is just based on the sheer fact that I don't give up. There are going to be things that are put in your way and they are surmountable. If you can't go over them, go around them. If you can't go around them, go under them. It's really that simple. I just don't give up."

Top real estate agent **Elli Davis** says, "Some days I have really rotten days. Everything goes wrong. Every phone call is a bad phone call. Everybody has bad things happen to them, and I think the most successful people are the ones who don't give up." Cobalt Entertainment CEO **Steve Schklair** put it this way: "Every project and every great idea has a million setbacks. If you quit at the first setback or the 50th setback, then you won't succeed. If you don't ever give up you will eventually win. Never, ever, give up – ever."

Don Norman, author of *The Way Things Work*, told me it's when he hits those boring, tedious parts of the job that he feels like giving up: "I write a lot of books and usually at some point I say, 'Why am I doing this? I hate it.' But you have to keep going, 'cause it's worth it in the end. That's true of all projects. There's always a part in the project that is dull and tedious, but essential. I just plow through it and take it step by step every day."

Electronic Data Systems founder **H. Ross Perot** said, "Most people give up just when they're about to achieve success. They quit on the

NEVER GIVE UP

one-yard line. They give up at the last minute of the game, one foot from a winning touchdown." Sleep Country founder **Gord Lownds** also finds a lot of people give up: "They have an ideal vision of something and they get to 80% and then the last 20% is just too difficult to do, and so they either ignore it or they walk away. Focus on that last 20% even if it's really difficult. Don't give up. Go the extra mile. It's the willpower and the determination and not giving up that makes the difference between success and failure."

The problem is when the going gets tough, even the tough are tempted to pack it in, but that's when we really need to persist. Like the other day when I was hammering away at this chapter and it really wasn't going well. I had a couple of interviews set up that were cancelled at the last minute. I couldn't get the quotes organized. My writing was even worse than usual. Finally, out of sheer frustration I shut down the computer and started to walk away. Then it hit me – I'm about to give up on the persist chapter. Is that ironic or what? So I did what so many successful people say to do – I didn't give up. I fired up the old computer and just kept going. I hate it when I have to follow my own advice.

Never ever give up. That would be my favorite motto.
Donald Trump real estate developer, celebrity

I just never give up. If it doesn't work one way, you try it another way. And you never give up.
Diane Bean VP business development, Manulife

Inside of a ring or out, ain't nothing wrong with going down. It's staying down that's wrong.
Muhammad Ali 3-time world boxing champion

STRATEGIES TO PERSIST
BOUNCEABILITY

FAILURE   MISTAKES
CRITICISM   REJECTION
NEGATIVITY PREJUDICE

They say successful people have thick skin, but based on my research it's more like they have rubber skin. They just keep bouncing back from failure and adversity. In other words they have BOUNCEABILITY.

Renowned venture capitalist **Steve Jurvetson** has Bounceability. He told me, "Failure stinks. I don't take it that well, but I tend not to let it get me down. The setbacks set you back, but I always bounce back." Medical research scientist **Eva Vertes** told me she has Bounceability: "When I do not succeed it makes me angry. But it's not something where I get down and I can't get up again. I think: 'Okay, that failed, so let's do it again better, and let's succeed this time.' It's being persistent."

Dawn Lepore, CIO of Charles Schwab, has Bounceability: "Resilience is important. You do have to be able to roll with the punches. If you're striving for something, things are not always going to go your way, and if at the first setback you say, 'It's never going to work anyway,' or you fall apart and don't believe in yourself, then you're not going to get very far."

When you get knocked down, how long do you stay down before you bounce back? I used to be devastated by failure, criticism, or rejection and mope around for days making myself even more miserable. I wish I'd talked to Chiat/Day advertising cofounder **Jay Chiat** years ago, because he knows how to bounce back quickly. He told me, "Everybody's gotta have failures. The point is how long are you going to remain depressed? If it's a week, you really have a problem. With me, it's about an hour-and-a-half max, and then I get on with it. The ability to handle your failure and continue on, without getting depressed or diverted, is important."

Switzer Communications president **Jessica Switzer** told me she has the same kind of Bounceability: "I'm not very good with failure, but I would rate myself very high on being able to bounce back from failure. I give myself an 'A' for resilience. I don't stay down for more than a couple of hours – not weeks or months." World-champion rower **Silken Laumann** says, "The critical point is getting up quickly every time we falter. Because the faster we get up, the faster we can try again, and the faster we're going to eventually succeed."

So, develop Bounceability. Then after being bent, pounded, stretched, and torn to shreds by failure and adversity, you'll bounce back to your original shape and recover quickly. After all, it's a lot more fun to bounce than crash.

> **I don't fret. I don't crash. I land lightly and then I go off again. I bounce.**
> *William McDonough* acclaimed architect

> **The test of success is not what you do when you are on top. Success is how high you bounce when you hit bottom.**
> *George Patton* famous U.S. general, World War II

STUBBORNOSIS

Another strategy to persist is STUBBORNOSIS. I know being stubborn is sometimes seen as a bad thing, but when you need to persist it's good, because it helps us hang in there and keep going when we're really tempted to quit. Renowned criminologist **Kim Rossmo** developed Stubbornosis: "I think stubbornness is a big one. You're never going to have a straightforward path, so you need to be able to handle the problems and the setbacks, and just keep going. I think tenacity is a really big part of it."

Moving from the crime lab to the science lab, medical geneticist **Josef Penninger** has Stubbornosis: "I think the most important thing is to be very stubborn. For one year, we had no idea of what was going on, but we just kept going at it and going at it and digging, digging, and we found some beautiful new principles of how pain is perceived. So you have to be very stubborn and many people are not willing to do this. It's not even believing in yourself. It's being stubborn and staying at it."

Musician/composer **Wendy Watson** told me that Stubbornosis helped her persist through financial setbacks: "Stubborn, my mother calls me. I do not give up. Once when we were owed money, I was polite for 6 months, but when they just wouldn't pay, I marched down to their offices with a good book and wouldn't leave until they paid me. I sat there and read for at least 6 hours – almost finished the book."

Stubbornosis is a big thing that helps me through those 26-mile (42-kilometer) marathon runs – especially the last 6 excruciatingly painful miles. By then my legs are carrying picket signs and threatening to go on strike: "That's it, we're outta here." There's always a huge debate between the smart part of my brain and the stubborn part. The smart part keeps saying, "Hey, there's no logical reason in the world to keep running." It's right, but the stubborn part says, "I refuse to give up." Stubborn usually wins over logic and that's the only reason I finish. Journalist **Michael Wolff** told me he uses the same kind of persistence strategy: "I think it's a matter of not accepting logic. The logic is that you probably cannot do it, so you may as well give up. Intelligent, well-balanced people probably give up. And I seem not to have that kind of logic."

So whether you're running a marathon, or jogging through the marathon of life, when you need to persist, call on the Stubbornosis strategy. It'll keep you keepin' on.

> **A certain degree of stubbornness is really good. Not blind stubbornness, but just saying, "I'm going to go for it. I'm going to keep on going."**
> *Patricia Seemann M.D., CEO of Sphere Advisors*

> **I had that stubborn streak, the Irish in me I guess.**
> *Gregory Peck Oscar-winning actor*

> **Hope begins in the dark, the stubborn hope that if you just show up and try to do the right thing, the dawn will come. You wait and watch and work: you don't give up.**
> *Anne Lamot author*

STRATEGIES TO PERSIST
BE IMPATIENTLY-PATIENT

BE SHORT-TERM	BE LONG-TERM
IMPATIENT	**PATIENT**
TO GET THINGS DONE	TO PERSIST FOR YEARS
DAILY	**YEARLY**

A strategy that will help you persist through the years it takes to achieve success is to be IMPATIENTLY-PATIENT.

On the one hand, successful people are very impatient on a daily basis. Nobel Laureate **James Watson** said to me, "I'm very impatient, and rather intolerant of people who aren't impatient when things need to be done. I like to move fast." **Michael Schrage**, MIT Media Lab fellow, said, "I'm a very impatient person. I don't have much of a future as a Zen monk." On the other hand, successful people also have the patience to hang in there for the many years it takes to succeed at anything. So they're Impatiently-Patient – very impatient on a daily basis, and very patient on a yearly basis.

Medical geneticist **Josef Penninger** is Impatiently-Patient. He said to me "I'm very impatient. I want things done. Be restless. You can never be satisfied." On the other hand he also said, "We work doggedly in the lab for 2 years making genetically-modified mice, and often nothing happens." So Josef has the patience to hang in there, and that combination of short-term impatience and long-term patience helped him make some big genetic discoveries.

Ben & Jerry's cofounder **Ben Cohen** is Impatiently-Patient. When I asked him what he was good at, he said, "I'm good at not sitting still." He's very impatient to get things done, but he also had the long-term patience to hang in there and make Ben & Jerry's Ice Cream a leader in its field.

Being Impatiently-Patient means that successful people tend to overestimate what they can get done in the short-term, and underestimate what they can achieve in the long-term. Nortel Networks president **Dave House** says, "I find when people set 30-day or 90-day goals, they usually don't score very well. They think they can get more done in the short-term than they really can. But when they look at a year, 5 years, 10 years, they are usually amazed at how much they got done in that period of time. I have far, far exceeded the goals I set as a teenager and in my twenties."

Many successful people echo the same thought. **Henry Kravis**, cofounder of KKR, says he also achieved a lot more over the long term than he ever thought he would. And he's another good example of how being Impatiently-Patient pays off. In the short-term Henry was very impatient and always "in a hurry to succeed, and in a hurry to prove myself," but he also had the long-term patience to persist and make KKR the world's biggest buyout firm.

So be Impatiently-Patient. It's a strategy that will help you persist on the long road to success. Okay, enough of this. Let's move on to the next strategy. Whoops, there's that impatience part. Guess I won't make it as a Zen monk either.

> **I'd win the impatience contest hands down.
> Successful people are always in a hurry. But you have
> to have the patience to stay at it and make it happen.**
> *Bob Ferchat* chairman, Bell Mobility

> **I'm impatient. I get bored easily. It's very hard
> for me to sit still. Yet, I can be very patient for
> something that I want.**
> *Lisa Nugent* cofounder, ReVerb

STRATEGIES TO PERSIST

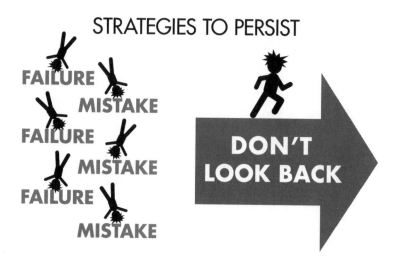

If successful people were cars, they'd have very small rear-view mirrors. They're always looking ahead, not back. The great architect **Frank Lloyd Wright** even had the rear window of his Lincoln Continental covered over because, he said, "I never look behind." The "Don't Look Back" strategy really helps when we need to persist through rough times. Acclaimed violinist **Adrian Anantawan** said to me: "In failures or discouragement, I never look back. I look back at what I've learned from them, but not the failures themselves. I look ahead at what I should do next." Renowned art gallery owner **Sandra Ainsley** says, "I always look forward. I don't look back. What's gone is gone. Just keep moving forward."

The 2 key words to keep in mind when we're trying not to look back are FORGET and FORWARD. First develop a really bad memory and FORGET the bad things that happened. "Failure? What failure?" General Motors founder **William Durant** said, "Forget past mistakes. Forget failures. Forget everything except what you're going to do now and do it." City TV president **Moses Znaimer** says, "I don't have much of a going-back memory. I don't remember bad things. I'm very future-oriented." Award-winning classical pianist **Naida Cole** told me she has bad performances all the time, but she forgets them and looks FORWARD to the next one: "You can't sit and dwell on them. Instead of thinking, 'I am so bad,' you think, 'What am I going to fix next time?'"

Yes, successful people are always thinking "next time" not "last time." Instead of wasting all their energy going over and over in their minds the bad things that just happened, it's a lot more productive to look ahead. Renowned basketball coach **Rick Pitino** says, "You must put that failure behind you and start to move forward. You cannot continue to linger in the failure…Yes you've failed, but now the question is very simple and direct: What are you going to do about it?"

The "Don't Look Back" strategy helped **Michael Jordan** become a basketball superstar. When he failed, he forgot about it and didn't dwell on the past. Instead he looked forward and visualized himself doing it successfully the next time. Real estate superstar **Elli Davis** told me she uses the same strategy when it comes to selling houses: "Sometimes I've worked on a listing for 6 months. I've done everything, torn my hair out with it, and I lose the listing. It does upset me, but I don't dwell on it, because negativity will really get you down. You won't be able to get up the next morning and smile and go out and do it again. I try to see the good in spite of the disappointment, and just go on to the next one."

So, when bad things happen and you need to persist: 1. DON'T LOOK BACK. Have a really small rear-view mirror 2. Develop a terrible memory and FORGET what just happened. 3. Put all your energy into looking FORWARD. It's maybe not a formula that will help you pass a driving test, but it will sure help you persist on your drive towards success.

> **I don't look back. I look forward. You always have to keep your eye on the ball that's in front of you.**
> *Janet Baker* CEO, Dragon Systems

> **Promise to forget the mistakes of the past and press on to greater achievements in the future.**
> *John Wooden* legendary basketball coach

STRATEGIES TO PERSIST

UNBALANCED
PERSIST THROUGH UNBALANCED TIMES

We're always searching for balance in our lives. But in order to succeed at anything we really need to focus on it, pour tons of time and energy into it, and give it all we've got. Which means the personal side of life – family, friends, entertainment, hobbies, sleep, and even ice cream (oh no) – need to be put on hold for awhile, and our lives become totally unbalanced. Then there's this nagging voice in our heads saying, "I really should be more balanced." At times like that it can be tough to maintain our dedication and commitment to work we're passionate about. So here are some tips to help you persist through the unbalanced times:

1. Remember, it's okay to be unbalanced for a while. It's more than okay – it's necessary for success. I know because I spent 10 years interviewing over 500 successful people and over and over they keep telling me how unbalanced they are. Billionaire vacuum cleaner inventor **James Dyson** said, "I've never been balanced. I'm completely out of balance and I think that's important." Whenever a successful person tells me they're balanced, I say, "Sure, you are now, because you've achieved success. But were you balanced when you were becoming successful?" The answer is always "No." Architect **Susan Ruptash** said, "When I was starting out I wasn't balanced, but I didn't see it as a bad thing. I was doing exactly what I wanted to do, which was pour every ounce of my energy into my work." So if you're feeling unbalanced, you're in the same club as most successful people.

2. Moderation doesn't work. Successful people do achieve balance, but not through moderation. They hate moderation, because it means going only halfway on the career side, and also going only halfway on the personal side. As Disney CEO **Michael Eisner** says, "There's nothing worse than the middle." So if moderation isn't a good balance strategy, what is?

3. Achieve balance through extremes. Successful people pour all their energy into career for a period of time and become totally unbalanced on the work side. Then they shift to the personal side, plunge themselves totally into it and become just as unbalanced over there. On any one day there's no balance but averaged out over time they achieve balance. NASA whiz **Dave Lavery** goes all out on the work side and may not see his family for a couple of weeks, but he says when he gets home, "I become obsessively Super-Dad and that balances it out." **Catherine Mohr**, engineering manager for Aerovironment, says, "I'll work my butt off for 5 months and then go to Alaska kayaking for a month."

4. We can't have success and balance at the same time, so it means making choices. What's more important right now? And looking ahead what will pay off more down the road – success or balance? Sometimes it will be success, other times it will be balance. For Charles Schwab CIO **Dawn Lepore** it was success first: "I chose very consciously that I was going to put work first for many years, so I didn't have my first child until I was 44. I made that conscious choice." Then she shifted to the other side, put family first and became totally unbalanced on the personal side to raise her child. Some people do it the other way around, balance then success. In reality, over our lifetimes we constantly swing back and forth from one extreme to the other on a weekly, monthly, and yearly basis. And averaged out over time, we achieve balance.

5. Be sure to keep moving from one side to the other: Success-Balance-Success-Balance... **Albert Einstein** once said, "To keep your balance you must keep moving." I would add, keep doing it long-term over time, and you get the best of both worlds: Balance plus Success.

STRATEGIES TO PERSIST

One more persist strategy is RFM – Relentless Forward Motion. It's a term invented by those crazy, I mean persistent, people in the sport of ultra-marathoning. This is extreme running, and I mean extreme, where they run over 100 miles in a single day. And they don't always pick a nice, cool, scenic place to run. They run in scorching, desolate places like the Sahara Desert or Death Valley. Just finishing takes incredible stamina, and the key to their persistence is RFM – they just keep moving relentlessly forward no matter how bad the conditions are or how awful they feel.

Pam Reed used RFM to become the first woman to win the Badwater 135-mile run across Death Valley. Other runners stopped for a rest, massage or quick bite, but Pam only stopped once to shake what she thought was a rock out of her shoe. It turned out to be a huge blood blister, so she popped it and kept on running. Pam said, "I don't stop unless I have to throw up. And I never did." (Gee, I throw up just thinking about it.)

RFM isn't found only in ultra-marathoning. Successful people in all fields have it. Sphere Advisors CEO **Patricia Seemann** works with many top executives in America and Europe and she says

RFM also works in the boardroom: "The CEOs I work with are just the last men and women standing. When everybody else has given up they just keep on going." Nortel president **Dave House** told me RFM helped him succeed: "When you decide you want to do something...pursue it relentlessly. I kept working at it. I just worked real hard. I kept at it and I didn't let up. I worked weekends. I worked nights. Persistence always wins in the end. Just keep going in a direction."

Chef **Michael Stadtlander** uses RFM to persist in the kitchen. I attended an outdoor feast for 200 people at his farm and he said, no matter what happened in life, he just kept moving relentlessly forward: "You have to be persistent. You cannot just give up. If you fall down you have to get up again and keep on going until you get what you want. You cannot give up." And that helped Michael become rated as one of the world's top 10 chefs. Baseball great **Hank Aaron** used a slight variation of RFM – RFS, or Relentless Forward Swinging to persist on the baseball field: "My motto was always to keep swinging. Whether I was in a slump or feeling badly or having trouble off the field, the only thing to do was keep swinging." And it helped Hank set the record for most home runs.

So when you're passing through a rough stretch, and you're tempted to pack it in, I'd suggest keeping these 3 letters in the back of your mind: RFM. No matter what happens, just keep moving forward relentlessly. You'll be surprised at how far it'll take you.

> **You persist even when there doesn't seem to be any hope. I say to myself, "I'm going to get there and I don't care if it kills me. I'm going to do it." And sometimes it very nearly does kill you.**
> *Ann Turner founder, Profile Recruitment Consultants*

> **Success seems to be connected with action. Successful people keep moving. They make mistakes, but they don't quit.**
> **Conrad Hilton** *founder, Hilton Hotels*

CONCLUSION

In conclusion, what's the really big thing I learned on this journey that started 10 years ago on a plane when a girl asked me, "What really leads to success?" Well, the really big thing I learned is never to sit next to a kid on a plane, especially one that asks big questions. Because you could spend the next 10 years of your life trying to answer the questions, just like I did.

I also learned that great people are just ordinary people. They have the same fears, problems, self-doubts, and shyness as anybody else. They fail, make mistakes, get criticized, and rejected just like anybody else. It's the 8-Traits that take them through it and on to great success.

Recently a reporter asked me, "What makes some people more successful than others? Isn't there an 'X' gene that the Oprahs and Einsteins of the world inherit that makes them great?" I said, "No!" Genetics has little to do with success, because many successful people, like Oprah, have no history of big success in their families. And many children of successful parents, do not achieve much success themselves. I've studied hundreds of successful people, and they come from different backgrounds and have different skills, but what they have in common are the 8-Traits. And if they have a special characteristic, it's that they do more of these 8-Traits than other people. They love what they do more than most people. They work harder and push themselves more than most people. They focus more and come up with more ideas. They improve more, serve others more, and persist more. It's not an X-gene that makes them great. It's the 8-Traits that make them great.

I also learned that "Great" is not a permanent state. We only maintain success and greatness as long as we follow the 8-Traits. But sometimes we don't, because we reach this thing called success and then stop doing everything that made us successful. I know because it happened to me.

While trying to succeed, I **WORKED** hard and **PUSHED** myself, but after I achieved success, I stopped. I thought, "Hey, I've made it. Time to relax!" And I slipped into my comfort zone.

While trying to succeed, I always aimed to **IMPROVE** and do good work. But success brought too much work, and I started saying, "That's good enough. Let's move on to the next project."

While trying to succeed, I did the little things that lead to good **IDEAS**. But then I stopped doing them because I thought, "Hey, I'm a hotshot creative guy and ideas should just appear like magic." But the only thing that appeared was creative block. I couldn't come up with any ideas.

While trying to succeed, I **FOCUSED** all my energy on projects and clients and ignored the money. But when I reached success the money started pouring in, and I became distracted by it. Suddenly I was spending all my time on the phone with stockbrokers and real estate agents instead of my clients.

While trying to succeed, I always followed my **PASSION**. But then I got into stuff I didn't love, like management. I'm the world's worst manager, but I figured I should be doing it since I was the president of the company. Soon a black cloud appeared over my head. I was very successful, and also very depressed. But being a guy, I knew how to fix it. I bought a fast car. It didn't help. I was faster but just as miserable. So I went to my doctor. I said, "Doc, I can buy anything I want, but I'm depressed. It's true what they say, 'Money can't buy happiness.'" He said, "No, but it can buy Prozac." He put me on anti-depressants and the black cloud faded a little. But so did all the work, because I was just floating along and I couldn't care less if clients ever called. And they didn't call because they could see I was no longer out to **SERVE** them – I was only interested in serving myself. So they took their projects and their money to other suppliers who would serve them better.

It didn't take long for business to drop like a rock. My business partner Thom and I had to let all our employees go. It was down to just us, and we were about to go under. And you know, that was the best thing that could have happened. Because with no employees, there was nobody to manage, so I went back to doing the projects I loved, and that was step one back towards success.

To cut a long story short, once I went back to following the 8-Traits, they took me back to success. But it wasn't a quick trip – I had to **PERSIST** for 7 years. But eventually business grew bigger than ever and we achieved more success than ever. And a little side benefit: once I went back to following the 8-Traits, the black cloud over my head disappeared altogether. I woke up one day and said, "I don't need Prozac anymore." And I threw it away and haven't needed it since (except at income tax time).

Failure's okay if we learn from it, and I learned success isn't a one-way street – it's a continuous journey. We just keep doing the *8 To Be Great*, because that's not only how we reach success, it's also how we maintain it.

Whoops, it looks like I've run out of pages. So until next time, I wish you well on your own journey to success, whatever that means for you. Be Great!

SUCCESS IS A CONTINUOUS JOURNEY

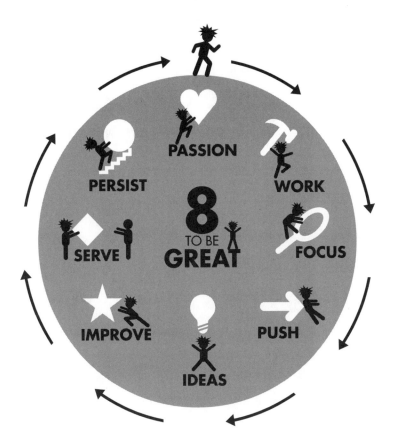

The path to success and greatness is a continuous journey. Just keep doing the **8 To Be Great**.

ACKNOWLEDGEMENTS

A sincere thanks to the hundreds of people who were kind enough to give me interviews. And a special thanks to the journalists, writers, and authors whose own interviews and words add immeasurably to my research.

Hank **Aaron** — **211** Original source of quote not found.

John **Abele** — **78, 79** Richard St. John

Dan **Aykroyd** — **23** Richard St. John

Sandra **Ainsley** — **126, 206** Richard St. John

Karl **Albrecht** — **149** Karl Albrecht, *Service Within: Solving the Middle Management Leadership Crisis* (Irwin Professional Publishing), ISBN: 1556233531

Muhammad **Ali** — **199** Original source of quote not found.

Robert **Altman** — **118** Roger Ebert, "No one else would dare make this film," special to *National Post*, December 21, 2001

Adrian **Anantawan** — **85, 206** Richard St. John

Chris **Anderson** — **74, 77** Richard St. John

Lance **Armstrong** — **133** Lance Armstrong, *It's Not About the Bike* (copywright © 2000 by Lance Armstrong), p. 49. Used by permission of G.P. Putnam's Sons, a division of Penguin Group (USA) Inc. **136** ibid., pp. 221-222 **139** ibid., p. 21 **179** ibid., p. 50 **190** ibid., p. 184 **134** CBC Radio news report, August 5, 2001

Linda **Armstrong** — **196-197** Lance Armstrong, *It's Not About the Bike* (copywright © 2000 by Lance Armstrong), p. 191. Used by permission of G.P. Putnam's Sons, a division of Penguin Group (USA) Inc.

Neil **Armstrong** — **195** Original source of the quote not found.

John **Bach** — **127** Jim O'Donnell, "The Stuff of an NBA Legend," *Chicago Sun-Times*, January 13, 1999

Meredith **Bagby** — **67, 78, 128** Richard St. John

Janet **Baker** — **44, 207** Richard St. John

David **Baldacci** — **175** David Baldacci, "An overnight success, me?" *New Statesman*, May 10, 1999

Jim **Balsillie** — **63** Sean Silverstone, editor, "Research In Motion's Jim Balsillie's Wild Ride on a BlackBerry," *HBS Working Knowledge*, special to MarketingProfs.com

Roger **Bannister** — **94** *Runner's World*

Bill **Bartmann** — **96-97** Adrienne Sanders, edited by Katarzyna Moreno, "On My Mind: Success Secrets of the Successful", *Forbes Magazine*, Nov 2, 1998. Reprinted by Permission of Forbes Magazine © 2006 Forbes Inc.

Diane **Bean** — **37, 81, 87, 199** Richard St. John

Warren **Beatty** — **37** Tom Hanks speaking about Warren Beatty, "Golden Globe Awards," CTV, January 15, 2007

Arthur **Benjamin** — **37, 46-47, 54, 76, 150** Richard St. John

Janine **Benyus** — **77** Richard St. John

Yogi **Berra** — **109** Original source of the quote not found.

Jeff **Bezos** — **41** Richard St. John

Keith **Black** — **21** On stage, TED, 2000

Adam **Bly** — **56** Richard St. John

Jon **Bon Jovi** — **19** "Passion is the key, Bon Jovi tells Oxford students," *National Post*, Associated Press, June 19, 2001

Liona **Boyd** — **135** Jane Haughton, "Conversations," CFRB Radio, November 11, 2001

Ken **Bradshaw** — **87** Courtesy of Nature, http://www.pbs.org/nature, a production of Thirteen/WNET New York

Richard **Branson** — **73** Richard St. John **86, 98** Cal Fussman "What I've Learned: Richard Branson," *Esquire*, a Hearst Publication, volume 137, issue 1,

	January 1, 2002" **86** Chris Anderson interview with Richard Branson, TED Conference, March 10, 2007
Craig **Breedlove**	**197** Original source of the quote not found.
Sergey **Brin**	**183** Richard St. John
Martin **Brodeur**	**47** www.harryrosen.com
Deana **Brown**	**198** Richard St. John
Robin **Budd**	**47, 82, 89, 128-129, 131, 168, 181** Richard St. John
Michael **Budman**	**41** Richard St. John
Warren **Buffett**	**39** "Eye," *Women's Wear Daily*, October 10, 1985, p. 10 **62** *The Wall Street Journal*, September 30, 1987, p.17 **67** L. J. Davis, "Buffett Takes Stock," *The New York Times Magazine*, April 1, 1990
Paul **Bunt**	**129, 165** Richard St. John
James **Burke**	**29, 105, 172** Richard St. John
Philip **Burke**	**119** Richard St. John
Charles H. **Burr**	**152** Original source of the quote not found.
Gary **Burton**	**55, 81, 139, 161** Richard St. John
Edward **Burtynsky**	**97** Richard St. John
Lise **Buyer**	**28, 108, 187** Richard St. John
John **Caldwell**	**68, 159** Richard St. John
James **Cameron**	**86, 95** Academy of Achievement – www.achievement.org
Russell **Campbell**	**22, 79, 162, 183** Richard St. John
Ronda **Carnegie**	**149** Richard St. John
Dr. Jean **Carruthers**	**111** Shelagh Rogers, "Sounds Like Canada", CBC Radio, May 14, 2002
David **Carson**	**29, 44, 177** Richard St. John
Percy **Cerutty**	**99** Original source of the quote not found.
Ray **Charles**	**92** Quincy Jones, *Q: The Autobiography of Quincy Jones*, (USA: Doubleday, 2001), p. 55
Jay **Chiat**	**36, 43, 176, 201** Richard St. John
Julia **Child**	**136** Mike Sager, "What I've Learned: Julia Child," *Esquire*, a Hearst Publication, June 1, 2000
Winston **Churchill**	**178-179, 198** Original source of the quote not found.
Peter **Cochrane**	**194** Richard St. John
Bruce **Cockburn**	**129, 181** Richard St. John
Paul **Coffey**	**129** Original source of the quote not found.
Ben **Cohen**	**141, 160, 205** Richard St. John
David **Cohen**	**42, 133** Richard St. John
Naida **Cole**	**206-207** Richard St. John
Ornette **Coleman**	**185** Original source of the quote not found.
Joan **Collins**	**184-185** Original source of the quote not found.
Sherry **Cooper**	**35** Jacqueline Thorpe, "Jazzing up the 'dismal science'," *Financial Post*, May 6, 2002
Ian **Craig**	**39, 132-133, 151, 162** Richard St. John
Russell **Crowe**	**16, 40, 133** Richard St. John
Ken **Danby**	**46, 91, 159** Richard St. John
Elli **Davis**	**19, 25, 73, 74, 120, 152, 164, 183, 198, 207** Richard St. John
Steve **Davis**	**173** Richard St. John
Wade **Davis**	**24-25, 40-41** Richard St. John
Sky **Dayton**	**106, 114, 177** Richard St. John
Robert H. **Dennard**	**112, 127** Jill Rosenfeld "Here's An Idea!", *Fast Company*, issue 33, p. 97
Daniel **Dennett**	**185** Richard St. John
Jack **Diamond**	**38, 168** Richard St. John
Thomas **Dolby**	**61** Richard St. John
Douglas **Dorner**	**87, 104, 132, 134, 157, 161, 174** Richard St. John
Peter **Drucker**	**73, 184** Nortel Networks Management Conference, October 2000
William **Durant**	**206** Original source of the quote not found.
Gerald **Durnell**	**161** Richard St. John

Martha **Graham**   135 http://womenshistory.about.com/cs/quotes/a/qu_graham_m.htm
Don **Green**   153 Richard St. John
Nancye **Green**   **29, 160** Richard St. John
Wayne **Gretzky**   **39** Original source of the quote not found.
Susan **Grode**   **61, 67** Richard St. John
Matt **Groening**   **31, 107, 148** Richard St. John
Bill **Gross**   **63** On stage, TED, 2000
Rudolph **Guiliani**   **109** Rudolph W. Giuliani, *Leadership*, (Hyperion, New York, 2002) p. 4
Aman **Gupta**   **27** Richard St. John
Paul **Haggis**   **179** Shelagh Rogers, "Sounds Like Canada," CBC Radio,
                             August 31, 2005
David **Hajdu**   **120-121** Stephen Cole, "Folk heroes, flaws and all," *National Post*,
                             June 12, 2001
Nez **Hallett III**   **35, 132, 151, 169, 175** Richard St. John
Gary **Hamel**   **112-113** On stage, TED conference
Suzy Favor **Hamilton**   **130** *USA Track & Field*, Suzy Favor Hamilton teleconference quotes,
                             May 22, 2001
Marvin **Hamlisch**   **129** Pamela Wallin, *Speaking of Success* (Key Porter Books Limited,
                             Toronto), p. 243
Graham **Hawkes**   **16-17, 195** Richard St. John
Goldie **Hawn**   **80** Richard St. John
Jerry **Hayes**   **26, 50, 84, 150-151** Richard St. John
Ernest **Hemingway**   **111** Original source of the quote not found.
Heath **Herber**   **165** www.highgain.com, Highgain: The Business of Listening
Conrad **Hilton**   **211** Original source of the quote not found.
Oliver Wendell **Holmes, Jr.** **103** Original source of the quote not found.
Lou **Holtz**   **51** Original source of the quote not found.
Dave **House**   **205, 211** Richard St. John
Robert **Hunter**   **173** Richard St. John
Pico **Iyer**   **120, 135, 138** Richard St. John
Douglas **Jacobs**   **159** Richard St. John
Janell **Jacobs**   **48** Richard St. John
Willam **James**   **152** Original source of the quote not found.
Anula **Jayasuriya**   **63** Richard St. John
Mae **Jemison**   **109** Richard St. John
David **Jensen**   **68, 74-75, 107** Richard St. John
Norman **Jewison**   **54, 129** Richard St. John
Steve **Jobs**   **17, 19** *Stanford Report*, June 14, 2005
Colleen **Jones**   **133** Robin Brown, "Inside Track," CBC Radio, January 5, 2003
Peggy **Jones**   **192** Quincy Jones, *Q: The Autobiography of Quincy Jones* (Doubleday,
                             USA, 2001) p. 224
Quincy **Jones**   **29** Quincy Jones, *Q: The Autobiography of Quincy Jones*, (USA:
                             Doubleday, 2001) p. 305   **59** ibid, p. 67   **88-89** ibid., p. 194
                             139 ibid., p. 67   **159** ibid., p. 303   **195** Richard St. John
Michael **Jordan**   **30** Mark Vancil, "Playboy Interview: Michael Jordan", *Playboy*, May
                             1992, p. 51   **39** Melissa Isaacson, "His Airness Shows He's Human,"
                             Chicago Tribune, March 20, 1995   **50** Original source of the quote not
                             found.   **97** Michael Jordan, *Rare Air*, (Harper Collins: San Francisco,
                             1993), p. 13   **183** "Air Jordan on the Air," *Chicago Tribune*,
                             July 17, 1998
Bill **Joy**   **91, 197** Richard St. John
Steve **Jurvetson**   **25, 66, 119, 200** Richard St. John
Dean **Kamen**   **54** Richard St. John
Mitch **Kapor**   **27** Richard St. John
Chip **Kidd**   **137** *The Onion*, June 2, 2004, volume 40, issue 22
                             191 Richard St. John

Nicole **Kidman**	**82** Lisa Gabriele, "Acting? What was I thinking?" *National Post*, interview from Britain's *Radio Times* magazine, Thursday, March 20, 2003 **93** John Hiscock, "Kidman carries on", *National Post*, May 7, 2001"
Chris **Kilham**	**72, 146** Richard St. John
Jeong **Kim**	**64** Academy of Achievement – www.achievement.org
Gayle **King**	**113** Kenneth Best, "Q&A: Gayle King: on Television, for News and Talk, Too," *The New York Times*, March 29, 1998
Kimberly **King**	**43** Richard St. John
Martin Luther **King Jr.**	**99** Original source of the quote not found.
Stephen **King**	**31, 45, 66-67, 81, 117, 121, 192** Reprinted with permission of Scribner, an imprint of Simon & Schuster Adult Publishing Group. Stephen King, *On Writing: A Memoir of the Craft* (copyright © 2000 by Stephen King)
Pannin **Kitiparaporn**	**115** On stage at the AIC conference in Singapore
Henry **Kravis**	**18, 205** Academy of Achievement – www.achievement.org
Kate **Laidley**	**51** Richard St. John
Anne **Lamot**	**203** Original source of the quote not found.
Kathleen **Lane**	**45** Richard St. John
Randall **Larsen**	**44, 84** Richard St. John
Jack Lenor **Larson**	**27, 29, 127** Richard St. John
Silken **Laumann**	**48, 72, 182, 201** On stage at the "Unique Lives & Experiences Series," Roy Thompson Hall, Toronto: Silken Laumann, world champion rower, physical activity advocate and author of *Child's Play - Rediscovering the Joy of Play in Our Families and Communities* (Random House), www.silkensactivekids.ca
Dave **Lavery**	**16, 36-37, 89, 148-149, 209** Richard St. John
Mike **Lazaridis**	**63** Deirdre McMurdy, "Research In Motion Ltd.," *Fast Company*, issue 49, p. 101
Norman **Lear**	**131, 167** Richard St. John
Dawn **Lepore**	**26, 91, 176, 200, 209** Richard St. John
Darlene **Lim**	**38, 83** Richard St. John
Brian **Little**	**17, 127** Heather Sokoloff, "'Funny' Canadian Professor Voted Harvard's Favourite," *National Post*, May 13, 2003
Jennifer **Lopez**	**177** *Entertainment Tonight*, February 14, 2003
Bill **Low**	**103, 141** Richard St. John
Janet **Lowe**	**20** Janet Lowe, *Bill Gates Speaks* (John Wiley & Sons Inc, 1998) p. 2. Reprinted with permission of John Wiley & Sons, Inc.
Gord **Lownds**	**63, 87, 162-163, 195, 199** Richard St. John
Jerry **Lynch**	**95** Runner's World Extr@, Friday, January 31, 2003
Douglas **MacArthur**	**197** Original source of the quote not found
Joseph **MacInnis**	**54-55, 167, 178** Richard St. John
Elinor **MacKinnon**	**67, 113, 121** Richard St. John
Margaret **MacMillan**	**18** On stage, Idea City, June 2003
André **Malraux**	**149** Original source of the quote not found.
Elizabeth **Manley**	**149** Lorna Jackson, "World This Weekend," CBC Radio, January 26, 2002
George **Martin**	**117** George Martin interviewed by Ed Bicknell, keynote for Canadian Music Week, Toronto, March 6, 1998
Linda **Martinez**	**92** Richard St. John
Jamal **Mashburn**	**93** Rick Pitino with Bill Reynolds, *Success is a Choice*, (Bantam Doubleday Dell, Audio Publishing, 1997)
Jennifer **Mather**	**17, 65** Richard St. John
Jaymie **Matthews**	**45, 60-61, 134** Richard St. John
T.K. **Mattingly**	**24** Richard St. John
Peter **Max**	**55, 134, 137** Richard St. John
Albert **Maysles**	**77** Richard St. John
Paul **McCartney**	**103** Barry Miles, *Paul McCartney, Many Years From Now* (1st American edition: Secker & Warburg Henry Holt & Company, 1997),

p.173 **135** ibid., p. 171 **130** *Larry King Live*, "Paul McCartney discusses 'Blackbird'", CNN, aired June 12, 2001

Craig **McCaw** **95** Academy of Achievement – www.achievement.org

William **McDonough** **43, 49, 72, 201** Richard St. John

Deborah **McGuinness** **57** Richard St. John

Murray **McLaughlin** **129** Richard St. John

Brian **McLeod** **131** Shelagh Rogers, "Sounds Like Canada," CBC Radio, November 14, 2005

Alexander **McQueen** **18** Bridget Foley, "McQueen's Kingdom," *W Magazine*, July 2002 **146** Courtesy of Fashion Television / CHUM Television. All rights reserved.

Rick **Mercer** **61, 84, 88, 137, 187** Richard St. John

Michaelangelo **46** Original source of the quote not found.

Ian **Miller** **163** CBC Radio, November 5, 1999

Wilson **Mizner** **41** Original source of the quote not found.

Katherine **Mohr** **209** Richard St. John

Tom **Monaghan** **62** Harry Beckwith, *Selling the Invisible* (copyright © 1997 by Harry Beckwith). By permission of Warner Books, Inc.

Louis **Monier** **55** Richard St. John

Jean **Monty** **138, 140, 163, 164** Richard St. John

Rick **Moran** **164** Richard St. John

Edwin **Moses** **65** Original source of the quote not found.

Walt **Mossberg** **89, 162** Richard St. John

Aimee **Mullins** **17** Richard St. John

Robert **Munsch** **24, 11, 137** Richard St. John

Story **Musgrave** **132, 136-137** Richard St. John

Debbie **Myers** **28** Richard St. John

Mike **Myers** **80** Original source of the quote not found.

Nathan **Myhrvold** **69** Richard St. John

Peter C. **Newman** **34** Richard St. John

Jakob **Nielsen** **158** Richard St. John

Drew **Nieporent** **41, 80** Richard St. John

Don **Norman** **57, 138, 198** Richard St. John

Dr Izzy **Novak** **19** "Say What?", *Elevate Magazine*, New Year, 2003

Lisa **Nugent** **205** Richard St. John

Sherwin **Nuland** **40, 57, 127, 153** Richard St. John

Erin **O'Connor** **74** Joan Lunden, "Behind Closed Doors with Joan Lunden," A&E Television Networks, March 23, 2001

Charles **Oakley** **109** Dave Feschuk, *National Post*, March 23, 2001

David **Oreck** **168, 177** Patty Kovacevich, "David Oreck Moves the Air," *Airport Journals*, August 2005

Larry **Page** **35, 57, 175** Richard St. John

Arnold **Palmer** **91** Original source of the quote not found.

François **Parenteau** **35, 155, 179** Richard St. John

Louis **Pasteur** **172** Pauline Barrett, *Success - Inspirational Quotations*, Four Seasons Publishing

Jimmy **Pattison** **37** Tetsuro Shigematsu, "The Roundup," CBC Radio, August 1, 2005

George S. **Patton** **61, 201** Original source of the quote not found.

Linus **Pauling** **103** Original source of the quote not found.

Gregory **Peck** **191, 203** Original source of the quote not found.

J.C. **Penney** **41** Criswell Freeman, *The Book of Florida Wisdom*, Walnut Grove Press (March 1, 1996)

Josef **Penninger** **56, 110, 139, 202, 204** Richard St. John

Irene **Pepperberg** **77** Richard St. John

H. Ross **Perot** **198-199** Original source of the quote not found.

Pablo **Picasso** **93, 112** Original source of the quote not found. **115** Picasso and ceramics exhibit, Gardiner Museum of Ceramic Art, Toronto, ON

221

Steven **Pinker**	**105** Steven Pinker, *How the Mind Works* (W. W. Norton & Co., New York & London, 1999)
Rick **Pitino**	**51, 93, 121, 207** Rick Pitino with Bill Reynolds, *Success is a Choice*, (Bantam Doubleday Dell, Audio Publishing, 1997)
William **Plomer**	**116** Richard Saul Wurman, Information Anxiety 2, *Que*
Colin **Powell**	**21** Many sources.
Lakshmi **Pratury**	**93, 141** Richard St. John
Marcel **Proust**	**109** Original source of the quote not found.
Gail **Prowse**	**149** Richard St. John
Isador Isaac **Rabi**	**113** Original source of the quote not found.
The **Raspyni Brothers**	**88, 148** Richard St. John
Cliff **Read**	**69** Richard St. John
Sumner **Redstone**	**18** Barbara Walters interview, December 1999
Pam **Reed**	**210** Scott Gold, "First Woman wins Badwater 135-Miler", *Los Angeles Times*, January 6, 2004
Ron **Rice**	**43, 108** Richard St. John
Keith **Richards**	**130** Victor Bockris, *Keith Richards* (Hutchinson, London, "Stones" by Kruger, published by Morpheus), p. 24
Cathy **Rigby**	**60** Cathy Rigby, "Ten Words That I Never Forget," http://www.souloflife.com/tenwords.html, September 12, 2004
Ed **Robertson**	**43, 87, 191** Richard St. John
Chris **Rock**	**40** A&E Biography: Chris Rock
John D. **Rockefeller Jr.**	**60** Original source of the quote not found.
Anita **Roddick**	**49** Anita Roddick, *Business as Unusual* (Thorsons, 2000), p. 31. Permission granted by the author, www.anitaroddick.com
Bob **Rogers**	**56, 121, 159** Richard St. John
Harry **Rosen**	**150** Richard St. John
Kim **Rossmo**	**57, 202** Richard St. John
Paul **Rowan**	**140-141, 185** Richard St. John
J.K. **Rowling**	**19** Marc Shapiro, *J.K. Rowling, The Wizard Behind Harry Potter* (St. Martin's Griffin, 2000) **89** Margaret Weir, "Of Magic and Single Motherhood," Salon.com, March 31, 1999 **139** Lindsey Fraser, *Conversations With J.K. Rowling* (Scholastic Inc, USA, October 2001), p. 21
Susan **Ruptash**	**26, 34, 55, 89, 128, 148, 208** Richard St. John
Stefan **Sagmeister**	**83** Richard St. John
Joan **Samuelson**	**85** Joan Samuelson, *Running for Women*, Rodale Press
Carl **Sandburg**	**23** Original source of the quote not found.
Ben **Saunders**	**21, 42-43, 73, 180, 197** Richard St. John
Forrest **Sawyer**	**173, 194** Richard St. John
Robert J. **Sawyer**	**192** Richard St. John
Steve **Schklair**	**42, 73, 198** Richard St. John
Michael **Schrage**	**204** Richard St. John
Wayne **Schuurman**	**50-51, 76, 115, 141, 165** Richard St. John
Daniel **Schwartz**	**152** Richard St. John
Gerry **Schwartz**	**131, 179** Richard St. John
Steven **Schwartz**	**75, 118, 187** Richard St. John
Albert **Schweitzer**	**153** Original source of the quote not found.
Patricia **Seemann**	**203, 210-211** Richard St. John
Seth	**81, 83** Seth, "A good artist must be torn between arrogance and self-loathing," *National Post*, http://peteashton.com/mirror/seth/seth4.html
Issy **Sharp**	**48, 65, 90, 120, 132, 146, 158, 160, 168, 190-191** Richard St. John
Lindsay **Sharp**	**65, 117, 153** Richard St. John
George **Sheehan**	**197** Original source of the quote not found.
Martin **Short**	**39** "The Ground Breakers", *Elm Street Magazine*, October 2001
Paula **Silver**	**146** Richard St. John
Peter **Silverberg**	**164** Richard St. John

Gene **Simmons** — **48-49** *Two Hundred Greatest Pop Culture Icons*, VH1, 2003

Sinbad — **120, 181** Richard St. John

Laurie **Skreslet** — **114, 134** Richard St. John

Fred **Smith** — **126** Academy of Achievement – www.achievement.org

Rick **Smolan** — **191** Richard St. John

Art **Spiegelman** — **114** Eleanor Wachtel, "Writers and Company," CBC Radio, January 6, 2002

Michael **Stadtlander** — **211** Richard St. John

Ringo **Starr** — **110** Barry Miles and Paul McCartney, *Many Years From Now* (Secker & Warburg Henry Holt & Company, 1997), p. 164

Martha **Stewart** — **10, 22, 34, 55, 113, 154, 167** Richard St. John   **150** On stage, TED 11, February 2001

Joseph **Sugarman** — **179** www.usdreams.com, The web's resource on ohe American dream

Sam **Sullivan** — **126, 158-159** Richard St. John

Leonard **Susskind** — **35, 103** Richard St. John

Donald **Sutherland** — **83** Barrett Hooper, "I'm Not a Redford Type," *National Post*, Wednesday, May 28, 2003

Jessica **Switzer** — **45, 161, 169, 201** Richard St. John

Amy **Tan** — **97** Academy of Achievement – www.achievement.org **126** Richard St. John

Bill **Tatham** — **63** Peter MacDonald, *PROFITeer: The e-newsletter*, Dell Publishing, volume 4, number 8

Freeman **Thomas** — **28** Richard St. John

Anthony **Tjan** — **157** Richard St. John

Rip **Torn** — **74** Scott Rabb, "What I've Learned: Rip Torn," *Esquire*, a Hearst Publication, May 1, 2001"

Amber **Trotter** — **95** Runner's World Extr@, Friday January 17, 2003

Charlie **Trotter** — **19** Ron Lieber, "Design - Charlie Trotter," *Fast Company*, issue 30, p. 250

Cynthia **Trudell** — **113, 181** Speech at the Sheraton Centre, Toronto, 1999

Donald **Trump** — **17, 199** "Donny Deutsch: The Big Idea," CNBC, June 1, 2005 **104** Original source of the quote not found.

Alexander **Tsiaras** — **194-195** Richard St. John

Kenneth **Tuchman** — **49, 61** Adrienne Sanders, edited by Katarzyna Moreno, "On My Mind: Success Secrets of the Successful", *Forbes Magazine*, Nov 2, 1998. Reprinted by Permission of Forbes Magazine © 2006 Forbes Inc.

Ann **Turner** — **173, 211** Richard St. John

Ted **Turner** — **34-35** Gary Smith, "What Makes Ted Run?", *Sports Illustrated*, June 23, 1986, p. 78 **39, 196** Peter Ross Range, "Playboy Interview: Ted Turner", *Playboy*, August 1978, pp. 70-74 **59** Maynard Good Stoddard, "Cable TV's Ted Turner: Spirited Skipper of CNN", *The Saturday Evening Post*, March 1984" **102** "Turner Vows Worldwide CNN as Cable's Coming Tops Edinburgh Agenda," *Variety*, Sept. 8, 1982, p. 96

Mark **Twain** — **195** Pauline Barrett, *Success - Inspirational Quotations*, Four Seasons Publishing

John **Tyson** — **38** Richard St. John

Jane **Urquhart** — **80** Avril Benoit, CBC Radio, November 5, 2001

Stephan **Van Dam** — **87** Richard St. John

Maurizio **Vecchione** — **88, 130** Richard St. John

Craig **Venter** — **30** Richard St. John

Eva **Vertes** — **60, 85, 200** Richard St. John

Bruce **Vilanch** — **111** Richard St. John

Roger **von Oech** — **181** Original source of the quote not found.

Marilyn **vos Savant** — **108** Original source of the quote not found.

Elliot **Wahle** — **164** Richard St. John

Sam **Walton** — **111** Original source of the quote not found.

Robert **Ward** — **23, 79, 172-173** Richard St. John

John **Warnock** — **194** Richard St. John

James **Watson**   75, 94, 187, 204 Richard St. John

Wendy **Watson**   202-203 Richard St. John

Erik **Weihenmayer**   25, 139 Erik Weihenmayer, *Touch the Top of the World* (copyright © 2002 by Erik Weihenmayer). Used by permission of Dutton, a division of Penguin Group (USA) Inc.

Jack **Welch**   36 Janet Lowe, *Jack Welch Speaks* (John Wiley & Sons Inc, 1998). Reprinted with permission of John Wiley & Sons, Inc. 102 Charles R. Day Jr. and Polly LaBarre, "GE: Just Your Average Everyday $60 Billion Family Grocery Store," *Industry Week*, May 2, 1994 130 Jack Welch, speech to shareholders, General Electric annual meeting, Erie, PA, April 25, 1990 148 On stage at the Seventh Annual Awards Dinner of the Work in America Institute 185 Janet Lowe, *Jack Welch Speaks* (John Wiley & Sons Inc, 1998), p. 78. Reprinted with permission of John Wiley & Sons, Inc.

Leslie **Westbrook**   73, 99, 113 Richard St. John

Ted **Williams**   131 Original source of the quote not found.

Bruce **Willis**   41 *New Idea*

Oprah **Winfrey**   42 "Joanna Powell, "I Was Trying to Fill Something Deeper," *Good Housekeeping*, October 1996, p. 80 94 Dana Kennedy, "Oprah: Act Two", *Entertainment Weekly*, September 9, 1994, p. 20 131 *Larry King Live*, "Oprah Winfrey Discusses Her Success", CNN, aired September 4, 2001" 185 Myrna Blyth, "Advice from Oprah," *Ladies' Home Journal*, February 1995, p. 10 197 Bob Greene and Oprah Winfrey, "How She Did It: Winfrey's Fitness Success Is Detailed in a Five Part Series," *St. Louis Post Dispatch*, January 6, 1997, p.1E

Sheldon **Wiseman**   37, 81 Richard St. John

Michael **Wolff**   203 Richard St. John

John **Wooden**   133 On stage, TED, February 2001 136 Coach John Wooden with Steve Jamison, *Wooden* (Chicago: McGraw-Hill Contemporary, 1997), p. 144 207 ibid., p. 80

Ken **Woodrow**   54, 191 Richard St. John

Tiger **Woods**   19, 64-65, 126-127, 177 *Larry King Weekend*, "Tiger Woods: A Golf Legend," CNN, April 15, 2001 80-81 Cam Cole, "Golf's favoured son," *National Post*, June 13, 2001

Hawksley **Workman**   130-131 Aaron Wherry, "He Just Wants You to Listen," *National Post*, December 22, 2003

Frank Lloyd **Wright**   206 Vincent Scully, Sterling Professor Emeritus of the History of Art, Yale University

Richard Saul **Wurman**   112, 130 Richard St. John 192 Richard Saul Wurman, Information Anxiety 2, *Que*

Sandra **Yingling**   19 Richard St. John

Babe Didrikson **Zaharias**   65 Criswell Freeman, *The Book of Florida Wisdom*, Walnut Grove Press (March 1, 1996)

Greg **Zeschuk**   35, 91, 133 Richard St. John

Zig **Zigler**   153 Original source of the quote not found.

Donald **Ziraldo**   141 Richard St. John

Moses **Znaimer**   206 Richard St. John

David **Zussman**   161 Richard St. John